PRAISE FOR *THE HIDDEN YOU AND YOUR LEADERSHIP EVOLUTION*

"*The Hidden You and Your Leadership Evolution* provides the essential foundation for effective leadership, whether you are a senior executive, an aspiring leader, or an individual contributor that interacts with others. To be effective, you have to first understand your own 'inner you' and be mindful of the internal drivers of those with whom you interact or seek to lead. Understanding both will accelerate your leadership effectiveness and business agility. Congratulations to Mr. Slone for dissecting and demystifying the toughest part of leadership, a topic seldom discussed in leadership books due to its complexity."

—Robert Saxe
Managing Director, nVision Consulting Group

"A must-read for anyone who aspires to be a true leader, a transcendent leader. John Slone successfully and elegantly captures the mind of his readers by addressing our natural survival instincts and human psychological behaviors that are often not understood nor applied by the majority of leaders today. Through his systematic approach to leadership transcendence of move, adapt, or left behind, John provides a winning formula that is essential to any leadership journey."

—Shaun Maine
Converge Technology Partners

"As an emerging leader to the world of leadership transcendence, John's guidance and education with *The Hidden You* is an eye opener. I look at the world and my interaction with people and situations completely different. I now understand the importance of influence, time, and transcendent leadership foundation described in this book. What's more encouraging is that I can see the results of this foundation both in personal and professional life."

—Pundari Pothini
Managing Principal of Advanced Consulting
Pivot Technology Solutions

"For those relentlessly striving to become an impactful and serving leader, John Slone provides detailed research to understanding your 'Hidden You,' along with an outlined approach tied with personal stories on how to embrace your life's experiences and opportunities in order to intentionally navigate your leadership-transcendence journey."

—Greg Billings
Senior Vice President of Services
Calix

"*The Hidden You and Your Leadership Evolution* is unique in its exploration of the physiological and psychological elements of leadership development. In the book, John Slone's concepts of 'move,' 'adapt,' or 'be left behind' capture the essence of the leadership journey. By following Slone's principles, every leader can foster organizational growth and leverage failures to build a confident path to ultimate success."

—Brett Bertz
VP Implementation Services, MedAssets

"Finally, a leadership book that focuses on the human-behavior factors related to becoming a true leader. In this book, Mr. Slone describes his own journey in such a way that I found myself literally nodding with confirmation as he addresses the unspoken DNA of a leader with clarity and cohesiveness that you will not find in another book."

—Jason Laffrey
Entrepreneur, Investor, and Philanthropist

"Slone has done an excellent job of creating a fascinating overview of leadership psychology that he crystallizes into three simple points, which he punctuates with engaging stories of two Civil War–era leaders. This approach makes it both a great reference and a meaningful read."

—Ajay Kapoor
CEO, TouchSource

"Slone's 'deep dive' into the Hidden You and the role that it plays in leadership transcendence is nothing short of masterful! It is a must-read for anyone aspiring to progress to the pinnacle of their leadership potential!"

—Edward R. Lyons
Managing Partner, AnBro Associates

"This is not a typical book on leadership; it is a compelling and insightful read blending science, experience, and emotion. A completely different way of looking at leadership and how you can excel."

—Denise Cox
Vice President, Americas Technical Services at Cisco

"During my tenure as a young manager working for General Electric, I was always impressed with the simple but direct message Jack Welch drove into the minds of so many associates. Jack was a realist and a very inspiring leader. I am very pleased to see that John Slone, in his new book *The Hidden You and Your Leadership Evolution*, has laid out his journey on leadership and provided a foundation for anyone who has a passion and desire to grow and strengthen their overall leadership skills. I recommend and encourage anyone who is looking for a refreshing and insightful approach to strengthening their overall understanding of leadership to give this book a read."

—Kevin Shank
CEO, Pivot Technology Solutions

"*The Hidden You* is thought-provoking and authentic. John Slone's talented and inspirational writing engages his readers on a one-on-one conversation that is real and intriguing. Every chapter is filled with nuggets of wisdom that unveil the surface and draw you in to see the underlying root causes of one's behavior and interactions with others. Here is a book that is powerfully poised to help one release the awesome leadership potential trapped within."

—Anna Leon
Canadian Vice President of Business Development, Pivot Technology Solutions

THE HIDDEN YOU
AND YOUR LEADERSHIP EVOLUTION

THE HIDDEN YOU
AND YOUR LEADERSHIP EVOLUTION

A SYSTEMATIC APPROACH TO LEADERSHIP TRANSCENDENCE

Steve,
Thanks for being a good wink in my life and for your leadership mentorship. Your endorsement is a true blessing and I am extremely grateful!
Enjoy the book!!

John B. Slone

BOOKLOGIX®
Alpharetta, GA

ISBN: 978-1-61005-916-9

Library of Congress Control Number: 2017912981

10 9 8 7 6 5 4 3 2 1 0 0 9 1 7

Printed in the United States of America

⊗This paper meets the requirements of ANSI/NISO Z39.48-1992 (Permanence of Paper)

In memory of my Mother, Mary Lynn Slone, whom I miss deeply. I dedicate this book to her. Without her love and support during the precious time I had with her on earth, I would not be the person I am today. To my family, my father (my mentor and the kindest man I know), my amazing sister (my angel on earth), and my loving children, you all mean the world to me. I am so blessed to have you all in my life.

CONTENTS

FOREWORD

With twenty-six years in higher education as a professor and administrator, I left the University of Missouri to feed my curiosity of becoming an entrepreneur leader in the public sector. At fifty years of age, I left a successful career in education to pursue an entrepreneurial career in real estate–franchise sales. In ten years I built a successful company with over $3 billion in sales, successfully selling my company in 1999. I am a husband, father, grandfather, airplane pilot, marathon runner, mountain climber, skydiver, writer, and speaker. I am the author of *Living at the Summit* and coauthor of the companion workbook, *Life Plan*. I have been blessed with the opportunity to be a coauthor of *Chicken Soup for the Entrepreneur's Soul*, and recently authored *Blessed Beyond Measure*.

Total success, right?

Wrong!

Even when I read the above paragraph, my innate response is to forget it represents my leadership, and I admire the success it represents. Then in a nanosecond, I reflect on all the trials and tribulations I experienced throughout my ongoing leadership evolution. Failures associated with my spiritual life, battles with health, challenging relationships at home and at work, emotional stress, the need for additional knowledge across various subjects, and the one subject that impacts all the above in one form or another, financials. My mind conjures up the many failures, moments of being left behind, and life lessons experienced along the way that led to my transcendent leadership, and an innate desire to share my life lessons with others.

In this book, John Slone does an exceptional job of identifying and explaining how our conscious and subconscious survival instincts impact our ability to successfully follow and lead others. As a foundation for strong leadership, which I desperately needed and would have benefited from greatly at the start of my leadership career, John confronts reality and touches on subjects that are often overlooked or missed entirely. So much of today's information and self-help teachings on leadership are conveyed through the desire to inspire, while incorporating little to no sense of reality as to why those inspired leadership behaviors are almost nonexistent today. The world is void of leaders—true leaders. Transcendent Leaders. The type of leaders who through a solid leadership foundation recognize leadership is a skill, and like any skill requires constant learning and preparation for what lies ahead. The type of leader who understands that to be a successful transcendent leader, they must first come to recognize their "hidden you."

What I most enjoyed about this book is that the subject and content is not seen through the prism of a successful CEO or a financially successful leader who once led a company to financial greatness, many of whom never practiced what they preached. Instead, the content is seen through the prism of a leader who through his own successes and failures within middle management discovered the need to move and adapt. Along his journey toward transcendent leadership, John experienced and confronted through curiosity the need to better understand what drove the type of human interactions he experienced. As we all have or will experience in different forms, along the way, John experienced what it was like to be left behind. In being left behind, John learned from those experiences, using them as a learning tool for future success, while increasing his value as a leader. Through self-actualization and now self-transcendence, John's knowledge, wisdom, and desire to help other leaders reach leadership transcendence through his systematic approach to becoming a transcendent leader are a must-read.

The world needs more transcendent leaders like John Slone.

Tom Hill
CEO, President
Eagle Goal Coach, Inc.

PREFACE

At some point in everyone's life, they will be presented with the opportunity to step into a leadership role. As an adolescent or young child, the opportunity could have occurred while playing chase on the playground. As a young adult, it could have been while playing organized sports or competitive video games. As an adult, it happens within the daily confines of the workplace or while interacting with family and friends. It's incontrovertible—the opportunity to lead has been presented to everyone at some point in their life. So how does human nature and society determine who gets to lead? Do natural-born leaders truly exist?

As a young man, shortly after graduating from college, I found myself in a leadership management role. Having to manage and lead men and women who were more experienced and sometimes twice my age, I was exposed to my weaknesses as a leader early in my career. Uninformed and ignorant of what it means to truly lead, I felt awkward trying to connect with others. I began to feel and observe the struggles that manifested within myself as I attempted to win the hearts and minds of those I was asked to lead. It was through my innate curiosity and desire to better understand leadership that my leadership evolution—the need to learn and grow through perpetual study and real-world application—began.

As I progressed, it was through various forms of success and failure, the element of time, and a perpetual appetite for learning new concepts, thoughts, and ideas on leadership that my understanding, appreciation, and respect for leadership has grown.

The Hidden You and Your Leadership Evolution is a compilation of leadership concepts, thoughts, and ideas I have gained along my leadership evolution. Along this journey, I have come to recognize that we are all born with the ability to lead. What determines this ability, and the opportunity to successfully step into a leadership role, is a set of complexities and subjects that span both the physiological and psychological leadership realm. My goal is to introduce leaders of today and leaders of tomorrow to a foundation of leadership concepts that are based on this reality. Throughout my leadership evolution, I have read books and trade magazines, and attended leadership seminars with the sole purpose of becoming a better leader. What I discovered was that most of the material presented was predominantly inspirational and built for a utopian world. I began to recognize that something was missing, and that there was a ginormous gap between how leaders were supposed to interact versus how they were actually interacting in the real world. What was being presented and encouraged contradicted what actually happens at all levels of leadership within society.

This book is about discovering the Hidden You. Before you can lead others, you must first discover both the physiological and the psychological attributes that define you. Once you understand who you are, you need a systematic approach to successfully traverse the complexities that human behavior and innate survival skills introduce. Through scientific study, contributions from physiology and psychology experts, historical figures, and my own intuition, it is my goal to set you on your own leadership evolution. The concepts and ideas I propose are based on my own leadership experiences from throughout my career. It is through this book that I hope to inspire and encourage leaders of today and tomorrow to identify with their own leadership evolution, and provide them with a systematic approach to reaching leadership transcendence—where your self-actualized knowledge and experience as a leader switches from being about you and your self-preservation, to being focused on the overall success and needs of those you lead. This is the highest form of leadership.

INTRODUCTION

The Hidden You and Your Leadership Evolution is focused on the realities of leadership. These include the inherent challenges within the complexities of human interaction, both consciously and subconsciously, and the social behaviors or social evaluation processes (how we evaluate the intentions of others toward our self-preservation) that influence our decision-making as leaders. This will provide you with a foundation of leadership knowledge and concepts based on these realities to prepare you for your leadership journey. To help you apply this foundation, included is a systematic approach designed to provide important leadership concepts and a road map for guiding you through your perpetual preparation and associated real-world experiences, thus launching your leadership evolution.

Rarely does available material confront the reality of your own leadership evolution and the need to understand, identify, and apply your Hidden You—your conscious and subconscious personality, and the innate instinctive attributes that must be identified to achieve the essence of true leadership, leadership transcendence. Instead, there is a lack of acknowledgment and understanding of how this Hidden You can impact your ability to effectively manage your followers, and how a systematic approach is essential to identifying and managing your inborn fears of being left behind. "Left behind" represents the moment a leader loses the hearts and minds of their followers, is unable to move the group or business forward, is denied opportunities to take on more responsibility, or worst case, loses their leadership role entirely.

Advancements in science and technology have facilitated a much broader understanding of our inherent human traits and what drives our social behaviors. To understand our Hidden You and become effective leaders, there are certain instinctive aspects of the human spirit that must be understood. As is the case in the animal kingdom at large, regardless of species, there are certain characteristics driving these behaviors that can be attributed to the basic tenets of "survival of the fittest."

This book will tackle both old and new concepts as they relate to our inherent survival instincts and how our conscious and subconscious social behaviors impact both how we are to be led and how we are to lead. Through this innovative and refreshing systematic approach to the leadership evolution, you get to decide whether the collective ideas, scientific theories, or hypotheses described in this book are relevant or have any application to the true nature of leadership, in addition to understanding the many social behaviors and challenges that manifest themselves when it comes to leading any business or organization.

As we explore leadership evolution—the journey you must take to reach leadership transcendence—we will examine the important association with the Hidden You and the systematic leadership approach to "move" and "adapt" or be "left behind." Through this exploration, you will gain a foundation for what a common leadership evolution might entail and what you can expect as you embark on this exciting journey in search for leadership transcendence. Like human fingerprints, no two individuals will ever take the exact same leadership evolutionary path. However, it is highly likely that as your leadership evolution journey unfolds, there will be forks in the road. With a proper leadership foundation, a Hidden You analysis, and a systematic approach, you can more effectively choose the most optimal path, thus invoking a systematic decision-making process that prioritizes both the self-preservation of the leader and that of those being led.

Being able to recognize that as a leader, failure and being "left behind" is inevitable. As humans, we are all flawed. No one is perfect. Within the conscious and subconscious mind exists an innate desire for individual self-preservation. It is when our own self-preservation is perceived to be at risk that our reactions to fear, and our innate conscious and subconscious reactions to fear, expose our greatest weaknesses. As a result, when making what we perceive to be the right choice or the right path, leadership decisions do not always lead to the most desirable outcome. Understanding this type of unanticipated outcome is critical to your leadership evolution and is an extremely important concept for any aspiring leader. A leader can make an informed decision based on sound principles, to include strong moral and ethical reasoning, and still end up with an outcome that is counterintuitive to the expected, desired outcome—an outcome that through social behaviors, group dynamics, and "group think" can leave a leader feeling isolated and left behind.

Humans are a complex animal, and over millions and millions of years have developed a complex brain that facilitates our ability to observe and reason, both consciously and subconsciously, all to help ensure our survival. It is through these instinctive attributes and our individual genetics that we develop our unique coping mechanisms for ensuring our overall self-preservation. These attributes that once ensured our survival on the savannas of Africa are now instinctively applied on a daily basis to ensure our survival at the workplace, within our homes, and within society as a whole. The need for group acceptance is as relevant today as it was a million years ago. In the past, being rejected by the group or clan could have resulted in a terrifying death. It could have meant roaming the savannas alone, a scenario that likely resulted in being chased by a saber-toothed tiger or some other predator.

Lucky for us, we are no longer being chased by saber-toothed tigers. However, the saber-toothed tiger has been replaced with other elements that conjure up the same inherent prehistoric reaction to anxiety and fear, often leading to behaviors that are less becoming and can lead to decisions that can only be deemed as self-fulfilling. Such decisions prioritize an individual's own self-preservation while ignoring the self-preservation for all. In leadership, this type of decision-making can destroy a leader's reputation and the ultimate goal of leading with transcendence. As with our ancestors, this type of leader is often destined for leadership isolation, where followers are no longer willing to be led and the leader is left behind, ostracized from the group and wandering the savannas alone with that saber-toothed tiger.

As a leader, it is important to recognize that as long as there is a hierarchy, which is inherent to our society, there is always someone trying to take your place. Whether that someone is consciously or subconsciously seeking greater status, the reality is the same. Therefore, it is important to understand that leadership is a skill, just like becoming a successful doctor requires skill. Through their own leadership evolution, a leader comes to recognize that there are certain leadership attributes and lessons that over time prepare you to not just become a leader, but a transcendent leader. A transcendent leader cares for the self-preservation of all, and in doing so can foster an environment where followers can tell you what you need to hear, not just what you want to hear. Mother Angelica (1923–2016) had the following quote: "Those who tell the truth love you. Those who tell you what you want to hear love themselves" (Skojec, 2016).

It is important to recognize that within the animal kingdom, there is no one species that uniformly interacts in a manner that leads to an environment built on trust and moral equivalence. Quite the opposite! All species are incredibly complex. Within these complexities is the inherent will to survive. Within the different species, survival is based on many different attributes, both physical and mental, all of which, in one form or another, can be found and directly attributed to the human instinct to survive, or as experienced in recent generations, the motivation and need to secure more "things."

In today's society, your basic needs and inborn discomfort associated with our ancestors' ability to survive through the collection and consumption of tangibles such as food, water, clothing, shelter, and fire has been replaced with the strong motivation and desire for intangible "things." Survival and discomfort are less about the tangibles, as these are now abundant and accessible. Today's survivability is more about the intangibles, the "things" you want that have no relevance to your ability to survive. "Things" could be in the form of material wealth, your title or role, your inborn need to be liked or accepted, or your desire to do the right thing. Regardless of the type of "things," "things" cause individuals to react and engage in predictable and sometimes unpredictable ways. Human survival instincts may have been suppressed over time; however, our natural, inborn reaction to our primary emotions of fear, pleasure, love, lust, pain, and anger have not changed much at all. The primary emotions within your subconscious mind, or your Hidden You, are what play a significant role in your ability to lead.

In addition to "things," personality, upbringing, and family system also play a significant role in your ability to lead. Beyond the day-to-day tactical methodologies and perceived best practices often associated with strong leadership attributes, there resides another significant subject that is often overlooked: the subject of human psychology and its relationship with the Hidden You. As humans, we have inherent survival instincts hidden deep within our brain. When these survival instincts are provoked or stimulated by our primary emotions, we are hardwired to react instinctually and without logic. These reactions are hardwired through intelligent design to ensure our self-preservation.

When it comes to leadership, there is no one way to lead, and no one way will always render desired outcomes. As you enter the world of leadership, and embark on a leadership evolution through perpetual preparation, you will realize that most available material regarding leadership will describe methodologies and techniques that are designed to create conformity and unison. Unfortunately, the unspoken reality is that in today's world, very few in leadership positions adhere to or even take the time to understand the various methodologies and techniques needed to ensure strong leadership attributes. Of greater significance is the lack of knowledge pertaining to the human spirit, and how as humans, over millions of years, via generations of struggle and success, our DNA and genetic patterns have been influenced and even changed entirely. Of significance is how these genetic patterns have impacted our ability to successfully lead others through self-transcendence.

Beyond methodology and leadership technique is the lack of knowledge and experience associated with the psychology of leading. The importance of recognizing the personality traits of coworkers or colleagues is rarely discussed or accounted for within leadership circles. Similarly, it is not often understood how your status and personality are observed and consumed by someone of a different personality trait or power persona.

The following questions must be asked or applied to leadership initiatives: What are the common traits and tendencies of different personalities, and how do those impact different tasks, whether as a single contributor or within a group? How does the ability to connect and influence the human psyche impact the ability to successfully lead and manage? What does it mean to connect? How does your ability to influence impact their ability to lead or manage? How does the subconscious Hidden You and the human instinct to survive impact personalities and communications as it relates to leadership qualities? Why should anyone be led by you?

This book is intended to answer the above questions and provide the foundation for new leaders, while also offering new, thought-provoking ideas for today's current leaders. Science and technology continue to advance at remarkable rates, and it is through research and insight that we are able to apply new concepts and ideas regarding leadership and its associated attributes.

Through observations associated with my own leadership evolution, and through my innate desire to grow, this book will introduce new thoughts and ideas based on personal observations and experiences to provide insight and answer important questions associated with why we interact in certain ways when leading or being led.

By understanding and adopting the concepts of this book as it relates to your leadership evolution, and by applying the systematic approach as it relates to "move," "adapt," or "left behind," the overall intent is to create awareness and bridge the gap between your natural, inborn self-preservation and your ability to lead others. The objective is to lay a foundation of leadership knowledge that will provide a new prism through which to understand human behavior and to provide a conceptual understanding of what is expected of a strong, capable, and transcendent leader. More importantly, this systematic approach of "move," "adapt," or "left behind" is to demonstrate that in leadership and within life itself, nothing stays constant. The world is forever changing, and the behavioral dynamics that surround you are always in conflict. Whether it is work, family, or friends, many of the same principles and foundational leadership concepts and attributes will apply.

Common leadership nomenclature associated with progress in your leadership evolution more than likely does not exist today. As part of the "move," "adapt," or "left behind" systematic approach to leadership transcendence, you will learn how to self-evaluate where you are in your leadership journey. You will also recognize that your current position can change instantly, and does not necessarily follow a perfect linear progression.

The following are additional questions to consider as you read this book:

- Do your current circumstances require new preparation and learnings to achieve leadership transcendence?

- Do you have the experience and knowledge to successfully influence others?
- Have you connected, evaluated, and compared your personality traits and tendencies with others?
- Does anyone take you seriously?
- Are you surrounded by leadership "turkeys" who lack leadership transcendence or any foundational leadership knowledge? Are you a "turkey"?
- Can your circumstances be overcome? If not, what are you doing about it?

Through my own leadership evolution, a journey that started over twenty years ago and will continue through my lifetime, it is my goal to share some of my own observations and experiences. In addition, it is my goal to provide a foundation of knowledge that will encourage future leaders to identify with where they are within their own leadership evolution. Through self-awareness and a systematic approach, I intend to provide you with the tools to proactively feed your leadership journey by knowing when you are effectively moving, adapting, or being left behind. Most importantly, my objective is to get you to recognize that your leadership evolution never ends, and that regardless of where you currently reside within your leadership journey, both success and failure are to be embraced as part of the journey. It's how you learn from your experiences, and how you apply your experiences to the move, adapt, or left behind approach that will help ensure your leadership evolution is always moving in the right direction.

Throughout this book and within the bibliography at the end are several sources, each having played a significant role in my own understanding of my leadership evolution, representing the building blocks for my leadership foundation. Although this book will provide a basic understanding of the necessary concepts, as part of your own leadership evolution, I encourage you to find time to learn and grow through continuous research. This will help ensure that you obtain via your own perpetual preparation the framework for move, adapt, or left behind, and how to successfully apply these and new concepts throughout your own leadership evolution. Leadership is a skill, and just like any trade, to become a successful leader, to become a transcendent leader, you must always be looking for new ways and ideas on how to improve your attributes and skills.

LEADERSHIP FOUNDATION

Good people are not those who lack flaws, the brave are not those who feel no fear, and the generous are not those who never feel selfish. Extraordinary people are not extraordinary because they are invulnerable to unconscious biases. They are extraordinary because they choose to do something about it.

— Shankar Vedantam

The Shankar Vedantam quote on the previous page helps lay the foundation for your leadership journey. In his book *The Hidden Brain*, Shankar, through scientific discovery and research, articulates and describes how our brain, what he calls "the Hidden Brain," influences and predisposes us to our hidden thoughts and subliminal reactions to events that trigger our most primitive survival instincts (Vedantam, 2010). It is through this understanding that we need to understand not just "the Hidden Brain," but the subconscious aspects of the Hidden You. We need to explore how our brain plays a role in developing our Hidden You—our individual personalities and interaction within the social evaluation process. Then we need to explore how our Hidden You influences how we interact and are perceived by others. These concepts will be an important step to ensuring a solid leadership foundation. Understanding how your life experiences and genetics shape your ability to become a truly influential and transcendent leader is essential to your ability to navigate the complexities of the human social evaluation process, which determines your acceptance as a leader amongst individuals or a group. As is the case with achieving anything of significance or substance, it's a process and not an event.

Leadership is a skill, and like any skill, it requires continued practice and experience, what we will refer to as "perpetual preparation." Within leadership evolution, perpetual preparation is the practice of continuously learning how to apply various leadership attributes. For comparison, we can use the game of golf.

Golf encompasses a systematic approach while incorporating a form of perpetual preparation that requires real-world evaluation (playing the game) to determine overall skill progression. In golf, perpetual preparation represents a relentless pursuit of perfection that requires consistent practice on a golf range, and a systematic approach that entails physical exercise focused on developing flexibility and muscle memory associated with a proper golf swing. Additionally, endless hours at a golf range practicing various techniques designed to improve on the different phases of the overall golf swing are systematically practiced in support of mastering various techniques that together form a holistic golf swing. As many golfers will confess, if at any point in time a golfer fails to consistently invoke perpetual preparation, the overall outcome they wish to achieve on the golf course will inevitably yield negative results. Like so many things in life, leadership is subject to the same consistent focus and pursuit of maintaining and developing new skills.

Your leadership evolution will take a similar path. A couple years into my career as an information-technology manager, it became clear to me that golf was going to be a work activity that from time to time was a way to conduct business outside the stuffy confines of an office. This was an enjoyable activity, with the exception that my golf game at the time could be described as a weekend golf warrior, a.k.a. "golf hack." It's not that my inherent athletic skills were not enough to become a decent golfer. My challenge was that my golf game was not developed as part of a systematic approach as described above. Instead, it was developed unconventionally, playing with my father once or twice a year, a man who too had never taken golf lessons, nor embarked on a systematic approach to hone his golf skills through perpetual preparation. My Hidden You, as it pertained to golf, was in large part a reflection of my father, who swung a club with such great force that there were times the force of his club hitting the earth was destined to show up on a nearby seismic meter, yet on many occasions the golf ball never moved from its initial GPS location.

It was through this experience and through self-reflection that it was apparent this great, influential man had subconsciously influenced my own golf game to resemble a form of his own golf identity. Leadership is no different. Our experiences, from the time we are born until the present, shape who we are and determine whether we will be identified as someone who possesses or has the inherent attributes associated with leadership. As we will come to better understand, possessing and developing leadership attributes as an individual is just one component toward achieving leadership transcendence, while understanding how individual leadership attributes apply to a given culture and overall social acceptance is another. Our experiences and inherited leadership attributes are handed down through past generations and genetics, absolutely shaping our Hidden You. Through Hidden You recognition, you will be enabled to better understand the complexities of human interaction, while also facilitating a broader understanding and need for a focused pursuit of the leadership evolution and the overarching need for leadership transcendence.

As a leader, it is important to understand that no one wants to fail. Each individual contributor or collective group has the desire to succeed. So, how do we as humans determine what is success and what is failure? The answer is largely determined by who is leading and the culture amongst those being led. At the end of the day, leadership transcendence is about how to effectively communicate and create success by systematically managing through a multitude of unknown failures. It is also recognizing that as a leader, you are always on stage when handling such failures, and your actions are consciously or subconsciously being evaluated by those you are leading.

Continuing with the golf analogy, in order for anyone's golf game to improve, you must understand what constitutes a successful swing. A golf swing can be broken down into several phases described as the takeaway, backswing, downswing, acceleration, and follow through. Within each phase there are a multitude of techniques and lessons that can be self-taught through individual practice or via a golf mentorship or coach. Just like leadership, there are several books, trade magazines, online tutorials, videos, and past successful representatives who are eager to demonstrate and share with the public why their technique is superior to another.

In order to lay the foundation for a better golf game, an important first step is required—you must first evaluate your own Hidden You. As we will come to recognize throughout later chapters, our ability to lead with transcendence—or in this case, play golf without embarrassment—is based on several factors. Some of those factors we have total control over, and others just happen within our subconscious mind. In my case, as a result of years of experiencing a bad golf mentor and then forming bad muscle memory, my golf foundation was severely unstable, or better defined as "broken." To build and enforce a better foundation, it required self-evaluation and a systematic approach across each phase of the golf swing, thus allowing me to leverage my strengths to improve on my areas of weakness.

Over time, through hard work and perpetual preparation, my golf evolution began to transform and I built a strong foundation. Through the strength of this foundation, continued practice, and help from a mentor, my game improved significantly. What were once weaknesses associated with bad muscle memory were replaced with proper technique. In some areas of my swing, areas of weakness became areas of strength. How I managed through those golfing failures played a significant role in my ability to sustain and improve over time. Often times, it required going back to a specific phase to retool my swing, to realign my muscle memory. It was also in those moments of failure that the game of golf provided for a humbling experience, and perceived weaknesses in my character were revealed.

It has been said "Golf does not build character, it reveals character." Leadership is no different. There is nothing more frustrating than mastering something, in this case an aspect of golf, only to later lose those skills and not obtain the desired results that were once consistently attainable. In fact, the game of golf is a good measuring stick for determining where you are in your leadership evolution. John Wooden, who as head coach at UCLA won ten NCAA national championships in a twelve-year period, is the one who coined the phrase from Heywood Hale Broun, a sports commentator for CBS television: "Sports do not build character . . . they reveal it" (Phillips, 1974). You can replace "sports" with any actual sports name and certainly with the word "failures." True character is revealed during difficult times, when times are uncertain, when your will and fortitude to overcome adversity as an individual contributor or as part of a group is tested. As we will learn, it is also during these difficult times that our inborn survival instincts play a subconscious role in how we mentally process, react, and cope with challenging circumstances.

In leadership, your character is not built upon one event, but a lifetime of events. Common attributes that define your character are trustworthiness, honesty, selflessness, will power, composure, and emotional strength. It is through recognition of the Hidden You and perpetual preparation that transcendent leaders continuously hone their skills and build upon these attributes, and similar to golf, create the muscle memory that facilitates their ability to achieve a desired outcome.

CHAPTER 1

THE HIDDEN YOU

The truth is incontrovertible. Panic may resent it, ignorance may deride it, malice may distort it, but there it is.
—Winston Churchill

As a young manager aspiring to become a recognized leader, it was through my own leadership evolution, my perpetual preparation and real world experience toward leadership transcendence, that I became aware of the many weaknesses and self-inflicted challenges I would subconsciously create for myself. Early in my career, I spent more time trying to analyze and understand why someone was the way they were than first trying to understand myself. It has been through my own migration and leadership evolution that I have learned how to recognize my inherent weaknesses. Then, via situational awareness and a developed ability to proactively adapt, I could minimize the exposure and unintended challenges my weaknesses would often create.

For example, one of my greatest weaknesses lies in my inability to effectively verbally communicate my thoughts and ideas. I discovered over time that I have an inherent ability to consume information and simplify complex issues so they become recognizable, achievable outcomes. On the surface, this would seem counterintuitive to my weakness. In my case, it turns out that both of these traits can and do coexist. The primary reason for this has to do with my audience, the disparate personalities for whom I am attempting to communicate my thoughts and ideas, and how those individuals process the information I am sharing.

Similar to how personalities can impact human communication, so does the way in which information is processed. Studies have shown that how individuals learn (process information), also referred to as their learning style, can vary. An individual will tend to have a dominant way of capturing and processing information, via auditory or written communication. To achieve leadership transcendence, it is essential to recognize different learning styles.

In leadership, learning-style concepts, entailing both visual or auditory consumption, are important to understand, as they refer to a range of theories that account for the differences in which individuals learn or process information. A visual learner prefers the use of images, illustrations, or written language to access or learn new information. An auditory learner prefers to learn new information through listening and conversation. Your learning style, or the preference of those being led, can impact your ability to effectively communicate. As such, the learning style theory proposes that all people can be classified according to their "style" of learning.

In this field of study there are various theories on how the styles should be defined and categorized. For example, in the United Kingdom, education after the age of sixteen is referred to as "post-sixteen." In a published report called "Learning Styles and Pedagogy in Post-16 Learning" (Coffield, Moseley, Hall, and Eccelstone, 2004), researchers set out to accomplish two key purposes. First, they wanted to expand upon what is currently known about various learning styles, as well as how different learning styles can impact a teacher's and student's success in the classroom. Additionally, as a fairly new concept, they wanted to more thoroughly examine the results of key models. What they concluded is that it matters fundamentally which learning style is applied to an individual.

Although the report was focused on determining the validity and overall effectiveness of various learning styles, the researchers concluded self-awareness and metacognition (awareness and understanding of your thought processes) are reliable and valid instruments to measure learning styles and approaches. In other words, they concluded that learning styles could be used as tools to encourage self-development, not only by recognizing how people learn, but by showing them how to enhance their learning. In effective leadership, it is important to recognize that how individuals learn, or their preference for learning, can vary. How learning styles impact your ability to process information is equally important.

Also important is the concept of a metacognitive approach to self-development and its relevance to the awareness and understanding of your Hidden You. As a leader, understanding the preference for how you or those around you process information is essential to better communication. In other words, there is no "one size fits all" when it comes to how we like to consume information. As this study concluded, one of the main objectives of encouraging a metacognitive approach to learning is to enable individuals to choose the most appropriate learning strategy from a wide range of options. Accepted amongst the many learning style–theories is that individuals do actually differ in how they learn (Willingham, Hughes, and Dobolyi, July 2015). It remains unanswered to what extent learning styles need to be incorporated into metacognitive approaches. Regardless of learning style, metacognitive approaches associated with the Hidden You are fundamental to becoming a transcendent leader.

Within your Hidden You resides your preference for how to consume information. When we incorporate that preference in combination with your personality, character traits, and social behaviors, any communication, whether simple or complex, can be a real challenge. To develop or create the most optimal communication experience, regardless of the means of communication, you must first self-evaluate your own tendencies. In order to be an effective leader, you must learn to be an effective communicator. However, becoming an effective communicator is easier said than done.

Early in my career, more times than I would like to admit, I would get frustrated with an individual's inability to absorb my form of communication. In these moments of frustration, the frustration did not point toward my inherent weaknesses. Instead, my frustration was directed toward my colleagues, coworkers, family, and friends, and in their inability to comprehend what I was attempting to communicate. What seemed simple to me, it turns out, when not properly communicated, was sometimes incoherent to others. Making matters worse was my inherent self-preservation. Through my own self-preservation and Hidden You personality traits, to include my overall body language unrecognized by me at the time, I facilitated a communication exchange in which I would come across both verbally and physically frustrated. This, in return, would cause the person I was communicating with to often reflect my frustration.

While experiencing such forms of communication, and upon reflection, there was something in these interactions and moments that was observed physiologically. In those moments it was hard to comprehend the purpose of the physiological changes taking place. For example, internally I might experience changes in my heart rate or my breathing patterns. Visually, I might observe that the person I was communicating with would get rosy cheeks during our conversation. It was clear something was going on, both subconsciously and consciously. How we responded to each other unleashed internal and outward reactions that were as unique to the individual as they were to the circumstance. As we will come to better understand, such communication and subsequent interactions are a form of self-preservation, and a component of our natural reaction of fight or flight, or stay frozen.

Fight is the need to stand our ground when under attack, and our instincts tell us we can prevail. Flight is the need to run away when self-preservation is compromised. Staying frozen is like playing possum, where the instinct to stand still, or act dead, leads us to believe that danger will find no interest in us and pass without causing any harm.

When it comes to leadership, my experience is an excellent representation of the complexities in communication that are experienced every day as we all interact within society. It takes strong leadership, instrumental qualities of enhanced communication, and a recognition of the Hidden You and its association with your innate survival instincts, your personality and self-awareness, your leadership genetics, and the basic tenets of leadership psychology by all participants to foster an environment that facilitates healthy communication and productive debate. The "fight," "flight," or "frozen" reactions referred to above are not leadership, and often lead to leadership isolation, where followers feel instinctively threatened or uncomfortable with the leader's desire to preserve their own well-being, and are no longer willing to be led. Thus, the followers develop a lack of commitment to the leader's stated outcomes. Hidden within this form of communication are conscious and subconscious reactions that prioritize the self-preservation of each participant.

To become a transcendent leader, the leadership-migration path must include an honest self-evaluation of the Hidden You. This migration incorporates a scientific understanding of our primitive survival instincts and the psychological understanding of both yourself and those you will one day lead. A critical step during this leadership migration is the knowledge and understanding of how to effectively influence those being led, how survival instincts can influence personality and character, and how psychological tendencies can impact those being led. Before you can lead or influence others, you must first understand how others consume and process your personality and inherent communication style.

What was once a fairly well understood and propagated message within the leadership-and-management community—personality traits and their importance to a healthy work culture—has over time been lost to the bottom line and relentless pursuits of financial results. In the animal kingdom, extinction can impose significant and sometimes catastrophic unintended consequences to the ecosystem. The near extinction of leaders, and the recognition of how your Hidden You impacts your ability to build a healthy culture and a healthy working environment, is having a similar effect. The void of transcendent leadership is leading to unintended social behaviors, which is leading to unintended work environments, where the consequences lead to organizations and companies getting "left behind."

To overcome such challenges, we need a renewed focus on leadership. It begins with the need to educate and share in the knowledge of leadership with others. It begins with understanding who we are as individuals through our understanding and application of the Hidden You.

CHAPTER 2

SURVIVAL INSTINCTS

The ultimate value of life depends upon awareness and the power of contemplation rather than upon mere survival.
—Aristotle

Throughout your career, it is extremely likely you will participate in or be the recipient of poor leadership decisions. During these experiences, it is not uncommon for these decisions to be in direct conflict with the overall welfare of the individual or group. Perhaps these decisions required a change in organization, which created doubt and uncertainty. Not uncommon, the decisions and undesirable outcomes were a result of, or in anticipation of financial trouble caused by a failed strategy. To make matters worse, it is also not uncommon to be the recipient of leadership decisions that are well conceived, rarely shared, and not properly communicated. If the previous examples were not enough to get your instinctive blood pressure up, experiencing leadership decisions primarily focused on short-term outcomes that benefit a small group of individuals vs. long-term outcomes that benefit the self-preservation of all should do the trick. If you have ever experienced such scenarios, the last few sentences were likely enough to trigger past anxieties, fears, and even anger, all of which are directly related to our primal survival instincts, which in turn play a significant role in our ability to lead with transcendence.

There is an epidemic on a global scale where the majority of perceived leaders are no longer concerned about the tenets of strong leadership, individual welfare, and the need to build strong cultures that ultimately drive successful outcomes that benefit the self-preservation of the collective whole on a long-term, sustainable basis. Instead, there is a laser focus on the financial results associated with what can often feel more like a back-of-the-napkin strategy with no realistic vision that with a little bit of luck and good timing, might yield positive financial outcomes. The notion that "It is better to be lucky than good" is no longer a cliché. Luck has increasingly become a common attribute across many aspects of our corporate lives, where a dependence on luck and a lack of leadership have created a tremendous void. Just as is the case with Las Vegas casinos, the odds are in the house's favor.

Having to rely on luck will invariably yield negative financial outcomes, where lack of vision and an unrealistic strategy often lead to a reduction in force, or downsizing, as per short-term "Generation Now" achievements that seemingly only cares for the survival of those at the top.

Today's work and financial climate is all about the now. The Black Eyed Peas summed it up perfectly in the lyrics to their song "Now Generation." In their song, they describe a new generation that, through the influence of technology and culture, must have everything "now." A generation and culture that not only wants things "now," but through generational instincts and subconscious self-preservation has been mentally programmed to feel entitled to all "things." Everything from easy money to faster technology, to social media collaboration and the instinctive need for acceptance is having a profound impact on this "Generation Now." "Generation Now," as the Black Eyed Peas so accurately described, has no patience, nor an acute awareness of what it means to create value through perpetual preparation, hard work, and the element of "time."

Tom Hill, a respected leadership coach and life coach, captured this vital concept regarding the need for patience and time that has been significantly lost within most leadership ranks. In 2013, Tom cofounded the Tom Hill Institute, an online program that provides all the necessary tools and resources needed to "Design an Exceptional Life." A concept, or tool, that Tom incorporates into his platform is called the growth curve, or the G-curve. In Tom's experience, as well as my own, it is at or around the eighteen-month mark that a strategy or plan, whether personal or business, reaches its full penitential, or a "tipping point." Tom describes a "tipping point" as "the site of critical mass resulting in a growth leap" (Hill and Russell, 2013). A realistic and well-thought-out plan or idea, when executed properly, will more often than not reach critical mass at or around the eighteen-month mark.

Although not scientifically proven, this is essential for all future leaders to understand. Throughout my career I have seen leaders and businesses make the critical mistake of trying to execute a business strategy or plan in a time frame, twelve months or less, that is not realistic. I have also seen where solid plans were abandoned too soon. Leadership transcendence requires patience and a realistic understanding of the element of time.

One of my fondest memories growing up was when I spent the day with my mother in her work office. My mother worked at the University of Florida in the College of Engineering administration office. While spending time in her office, watching her interact and communicate with various individuals, there was a process that always caught my attention. Every so often, a person would walk into her office and place a manila envelope in a bin on her desk. My mother would open the manila envelope, remove and read through its contents, then take her time in either writing or typing up a communication. She would then take her completed communication and place it back in the manila envelope. Just before she placed the envelope in an outbox bin on her desk, she would sign and write the date and time on the front of the envelope for tracking purposes.

What a remarkable process. Even at my young age, I could recognize that whatever was happening was important to the individuals involved. What's most remarkable is that what I witnessed at a young age was how communication most often took place before the invention of the internet and e-mail. Back in those days, it took time and patience to perform such critical communication tasks, where proper acknowledgments via time-and-date stamps were essential to accountability. Through reflection, I can recognize how this manual process facilitated a culture of communication that required an almost subconscious acceptance of time and space that required a high degree of patience. As a result, communication was much slower than it is today, and yet arguably more effective and less disruptive.

In addition to e-mail, the smartphone is another technology that has significantly changed our culture. With the smartphone, information is at our fingertips. What once required a trip to the library, looking through a card catalog to find a book or subject, then reading the book or subject to obtain information, is now instantly available. What took hours or days now takes minutes. Our ability to communicate has gone virtual. No longer is it required to go to an office to get work done. With wireless technology, smartphones, and the Internet, you can be anywhere in the world and still communicate instantly. (Notice how I did not state "effectively.")

Combined, these technologies have changed the way in which we communicate. We are far more efficient, which has improved many aspects of our lives. However, like most things in life, change, whether good or bad, can have unintended consequences. In this case, advancement in technology has changed our culture. It has rewired our brains, both consciously and subconsciously.

As a result of "Generation Now," today's culture is vastly different than my time spent in my mother's work office. No longer is patience a virtue. In fact, patience left the building as soon as the Internet and e-mail replaced the old, manual system. Technology has significantly changed our culture, our instinctive behaviors, and our ability to lead with transcendence.

Similar to how advancement in technology has impacted our behaviors, it is also accelerating our understanding of the sciences. These advancements provide greater insight into the inner workings of things such as the human brain and how conscious and subconscious thoughts associated with our survival instincts and self-preservation directly impact how we, as leaders and in being led, process and react to different circumstances and situations. These circumstances and experiences happen over a lifetime. Indirectly and directly, they shape our individual character and overall personality traits that impact our ability to effectively communicate and, through transcendence, lead others. It is through recent scientific studies and advancements in magnetic resonance imaging (MRI) technology that scientists can better understand how certain functions of our brain play an intricate role in our survival, and how our survival instincts shape the way we process and successfully communicate with others. Successful human interactions are highly dependent upon how we communicate. It is how we communicate that determines the success of our interactions and in our ability to connect.

Through the insight provided by Shankar Vedantam's book *The Hidden Brain*, Robert Winston's *Human Instinct*, and Marc Schoen's *Your Survival Instinct Is Killing You*, technology and advances in science are changing the landscape and broadening our understanding of the human brain and our inborn survival instincts (Vedantam, 2010) (Winston, 2002) (Schoen, 2013). Over the course of millions of years, humans have evolved to ensure the survival of our species. As part of this human evolution, it is the development of our brain that has been most essential to our self-preservation. Just as our leadership foundation must evolve, our brain had to evolve, building upon a foundation of survival instincts that, over millions of years, has allowed the human race to get to the top, and stay there (a.k.a. the food chain!). Through modern science, we can now better understand how these changes facilitated our survival, both in the past and in the present. A lot has changed over this enormous period of time, and as humans, our brain and our physiological attributes have changed with it, impacting how we deal with these drastic changes from a rational, emotional, and instinctive perspective.

Across the modern scientific community, it is well understood and accepted that it is not physical attributes that place humans atop the food chain; it is through our ability to reason. Just as our ancestors traversed the savannas of South Africa, leveraging their survival instincts to avoid being eaten, these same survival instincts are encoded in our DNA, subconsciously being invoked to ensure our day-to-day survival and self-preservation. It is through our subconscious survival instincts and our new understandings of its existence that we now can leverage this new knowledge to better understand how these inherent attributes shape our character, our personalities, and our ability to communicate, and ultimately become a transcendent leader.

For example, fear associated with financial instability will inherently influence your ability to lead. Like food, physiologically, money is a tangible asset associated with survival. As such, it has a high probability of influencing how you make decisions that impact your self-preservation and the self-preservation of others.

Unfortunately or fortunately, based on your perspective, until you actually experience personal financial hardship, the opportunity to learn and grow from such an experience, with the ability to recognize how such a circumstance impacts the ability to reach leadership transcendence, is hard to ascertain. Maintaining a financially stable lifestyle will help keep those inborn fears at bay. Alternatively, financial instability can destroy your ability to lead with transcendence, often leading to deceit and deception.

Financial instability creates a leader who is less focused on their leadership evolution and more focused on money. Financial instability also lends itself to social behaviors where leaders are more likely to steal from an organization and its people, not just money, but from the self-preservation and goodwill of all. Transcendent leaders manage their personal finances with the same focus, scrutiny, and effort they apply to their team. Any alternative will only lead to and represent an emotionally detached, ineffective leader.

To better understand how things like financial instability can impact our survival instincts and their association with transcendent leadership, we need to use modern science and its contribution to neuroscience to first understand how the human brain predisposes us to interact within the world around us and within society at large.

The human brain is a complex organ that evolved over time. Each major component developed sequentially, one on top of the other. Representing three distinct components, each component developed over time to enhance and facilitate our chances for overall survival.

The oldest, most primitive part of our brain is located within the brain stem, or what is also known as the cerebellum. The brain stem is sometimes referred to in the scientific community as the reptilian part of our brain, which represents the most prehistoric part of the brain. It is this part of our brain that cares for the most basic functions of our brain and is important to our vital functions, as it receives direct communications from our entire body via the spinal cord and central nervous system. Examples of these vital functions would be our breathing, heartbeat, and overall blood pressure. A vital function of the brain stem is the activation of our fight-or-flight response system. The brain stem is also involved in caring for our body's overall movement. More importantly, the brain stem is relatively emotionless and automatically prioritizes self-preservation.

As our brains continued to evolve, we developed a second component of our brain, referred to as the limbic brain system. As part of this progression, the limbic brain system developed on top of the brain stem, allowing it to receive communications directly from the brain stem, where it can attach coded emotions to these communications in the form of nerve impulses. A nerve impulse is the way nerve cells (neurons) communicate with one another. Similar to the brain stem, the limbic brain system's functions are automatic or instinctive, and often lack awareness.

The third portion of the developed brain and arguably the most essential to our self-preservation is the cerebral cortex. The cerebral cortex developed on top of the limbic brain system and plays a key role in memory, attention, perception, awareness, thought, language, and consciousness. Humans, being mammals, have the largest cerebral cortex relative to the size of their brains. The number of neurons within a mammal's cerebral cortex and their relative abundance as compared to different parts of the brain is what determines the species' overall neural function and intellectual behavior. Only the long-finned pilot whale, a species of dolphin, has more neocortical neurons than any mammal studied to date, including humans. Within mammals, the larger the cerebral cortex, the more complex the patterns of organization and other advanced capabilities. This is important, as the development of the cerebral cortex and our understanding of the three components of the brain have facilitated our ability to better understand and control limbic impulses. This understanding facilitates our ability to better control our emotional reactions to our inborn survival instincts.

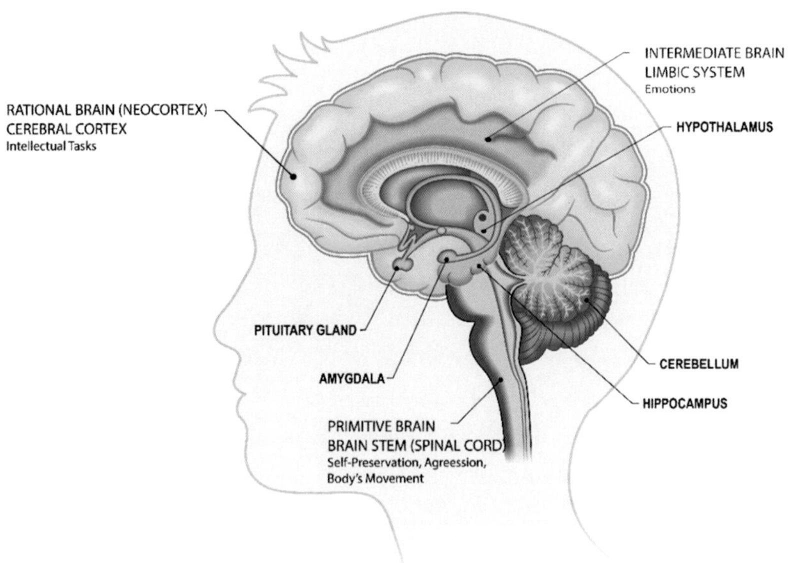

The interaction that occurs within these three distinct components continue to develop to this day. These interactions occur mostly within the cerebral cortex, which plays a critical role in self-preservation, as it attempts to insert control over the older, more primitive components of the brain. "Attempt" is the operative word, as the cerebral cortex and the limbic system are somewhat autonomous, often inherently driven to assert control over one another. Naturally, the cerebral cortex tries to assert its authority, while the limbic system is more instinctive and quick to dismiss the cerebral cortex's attempts to control it.

As this scenario within the brain plays out every day, there are certain attributes associated with this progression that, without knowledge, can compromise our ability to effectively communicate with and successfully lead others. Through adaptation, our brain intends to insert a top-down approach in its attempt to control its more primitive functions. Depending on your view of evolution or creationism, the sequence in which our brains have developed or arrived on earth via intelligent design is extremely unique and borderline sinister in its function. For example, the lower or more primitive functions have greater control of our physical and emotional attributes, which creates a constant struggle between the limbic system and the cerebral components of the brain. Two-way communication does not exist between the limbic system and the cerebral cortex. Communication only traverses up, from the limbic system to the cerebral cortex. The result is a constant tug-of-war, both consciously and subconsciously in our minds, which plays out every day, producing both comfort and discomfort as we interact within society.

As a result of the innate conflict of caring for your own self-preservation while also leading others, the likelihood of experiencing a situation that initiates this internal tug-of-war is highly probable. At some point in time as an individual contributor (or transcendent follower) or as a future leader, you will face unique challenges that will severely test your ability to allow reason to overcome the primitive nature of your limbic system. Although rarely discussed for fear of judgment and as an oxymoron to what society defines as leadership, many leaders experience leadership outcomes that lead to depression, anxiety, and/or fear of failure. As part of your leadership evolution, understanding how our brain was developed and how it impacts our ability to lead with transcendence is essential. Without this knowledge, the potential for experiencing a mental breakdown (also known as a nervous breakdown) is highly probable.

Wikipedia describes a mental breakdown as an acute, time-limited mental disorder that manifests primarily as severe stress-induced depression, anxiety, or dissociation in a previously functional individual, to the extent that they are no longer able to function on a day-to-day basis until the disorder is resolved. It is defined by its temporary nature, and often closely tied to psychological burnout, severe overwork, sleep deprivation, and similar stressors, which may combine to temporarily overwhelm an individual with otherwise sound mental functions (Wikipedia, Mental Breakdown, n.d.).

Now, many of you are thinking, Th*at would not happen to me, I am of strong mind*. I too once held a similar belief. As you can probably guess, I was completely wrong. For me, my mental breakdown occurred when I changed jobs. Having spent several years with my previous employer, my comfort level and overall confidence was at an all-time high. Upon joining a new company, I was thrust into what I perceived to be a high-stress, high-anxiety, and fearful situation. My stress was driven by my fear of failure—the unintended consequence of failure and its impact on my family system as a sole provider.

As a result, my limbic system kicked in and my primal survival instincts took over. I was in fight, flight, or frozen mode. In this situation, my brain went into frozen mode. My cerebral analysis failed to take control. My cerebral analysis failed to execute. As a result, I went into a limbic-system tailspin. My anxiety and fear took control, and as described above, I was no longer able to function with a sense of clarity. It took several days and help from a psychiatrist for me to recognize and better understand what caused such a circumstance, and how to successfully overcome and cope with such an experience. All in all, this experience had a profound impact on my new understanding of the human brain, and as part of my perpetual preparation, led me to seek further knowledge on what would cause a mental breakdown of this kind.

In the world of leadership, how we understand and cope with these subconscious impulses and their association with emotions such as comfort and discomfort, or fear and anger, is extremely important. Have you ever walked up on a snake and felt an automatic and reflexive response that permeated throughout your entire physical body in the form of flight, fight, or frozen? Understanding how the brain stem, the limbic system, and the cerebral cortex work together to ensure your self-preservation is an important step in being able to identify the Hidden You, and for putting yourself on a path toward leadership transcendence.

Limbic impulses come from the brain stem, reacting quickly. They attach primal emotions to nerve impulses that have been initiated within the physical body to ensure your self-preservation. To understand how such impulses impact the Hidden You, it is important to recognize that when these primitive emotions resonate within the physical body, they are pure and with intent. They resonate within the nervous system, traversing through the brain stem, making their way to the limbic system. They traverse this path without receiving any cerebral analysis. Have you ever wondered why individuals, or perhaps yourself, get nervous about an upcoming public-speaking event or a public performance? A reason for this outcome is that the limbic system has a strong connection to the automatic nervous and endocrine system, and without proper cerebral analysis and interpretation, the limbic system will send automatic impulses to areas of the physical body that are geared toward self-preservation.

The limbic system is made up of several parts, which include hard-to-pronounce names like the hypothalamus, the hippocampus (associated with learning and memory), the amygdala, and basal ganglia (which contains the nucleus accumbens and the ventral tegmental area (VTA)). Combined, these areas represent the portion of the brain where pleasure and fear originate, where an instinctive positive reaction to pleasure or a negative reaction to anxiety collide. For our purpose, we do not need to know all the details regarding these components, only how together they impact our physical and emotional responses.

It is within the limbic system where modern science has discovered the actual physical and emotional basis for primal experiences such as pain, hunger, anger, fear, and pleasure. All of these impact society at large, and through human interactions and social behaviors, drive the human body's chemical reactions that ensure self-preservation. Under the influence of pleasure, and via the limbic system's direct connection to the neurotransmitter called dopamine, these reactions will release the natural opiates found in the brain called endorphins. Dopamine is a chemical produced by the brain that influences our habits and addictions, while endorphins influence how our habits and addictions are experienced. This is especially true when it comes to experiencing pleasure.

When it comes to pleasure, these chemicals interact with other parts of the brain in such a significant way that our brain encourages us to seek the stimulus creating this pleasurable sensation. This pleasure can resonate in the form of physical or emotional reactions. When we interact with someone not just in a platonic way, but in a way where we truly connect, our dopamine surges and we feel a rush of euphoria and acceptance. Once this occurs, our dopamine levels will subside and begin to drop. However, this chemical event is not forgotten and is hardwired into our brain. The late psychologist Donald Hebb is a Canadian neuropsychologist known for his work in the field of associative learning who coined the phrase "Neurons that fire together, wire together" (Hebb, 1949). In this coined phrase, Hebb captures the essence of how every experience, thought, feeling, and physical sensation, when repeated over and over, the brain learns to trigger the same neurons each time. Simply put, two things that occur within the brain become embedded within the brain. When two sets of neurons are triggered simultaneously, even if originally they were two separate events, the relationship between these neural networks can become wired together. This is one of the reasons why our ability to recall pleasurable and painful events is far easier than remembering how to do algebra from college.

It is this process that leads to the controlling of all future impulses and what becomes a single set of conjoined neurons. As part of our desire for more pleasure, we anticipate the next encounter, and in anticipation of our next encounter, our dopamine levels surge. In the case of pleasure, we embrace its existence and often overlook the significance of what has become hardwired into our brain. Sometimes to our own detriment, as eventual withdrawal sets in, these pleasures and desires can lead to addictions. Thus, this raises our awareness of how something pleasurable can become a possible detriment to our overall survival and self-preservation.

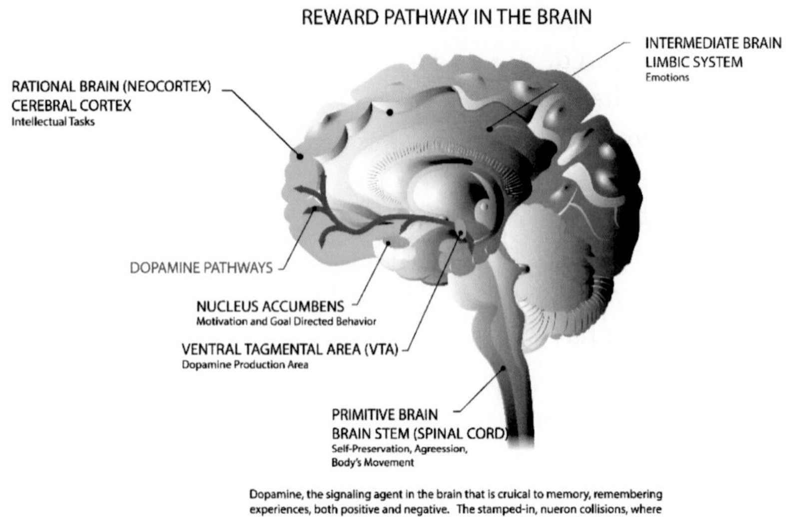

Dopamine, the signaling agent in the brain that is cruical to memory, remembering experiences, both positive and negative. The stamped-in, nueron collisions, where motivation to repeat pleasureable experiences begin.

As it pertains to becoming a transcendent leader, we would certainly embrace addictions related to building strong work cultures, where each contributor is encouraged and committed to the success of the team. As a transcendent leader, you can foster an environment where people connect, where vision, strategy, and culture come together as one, where our collective dopamine levels rise, and where the commitment to the self-preservation of all leads to the most optimal intended outcome.

Unfortunately, our brains are not wired to sustain such high levels of dopamine, nor is obtaining such a utopian culture likely. As Sir Isaac Newton's third law of motion states, "To every action there is always opposed on equal reaction" (Newton, 1846, p.

83). In a perfect world, this purpose or goal would be the most ideal state, the ultimate leadership achievement. However, our self-preservation and subsequent neural impulses subconsciously, or in some cases consciously, work in direct conflict with such goals. Just as our brain seeks to impose a top-down approach to control the more primitive functions of our brain, as humans, we are predisposed to the concept of hierarchy.

Throughout the animal kingdom, hierarchy plays a significant role in how each species communicates, which ultimately plays a significant role in determining which form of species survives. This dynamic has occurred over billions of years and continues today. But what is driving this behavior? Modern science has given us greater insight into the relationship of our primal experiences that include pain, hunger, anger, fear, and pleasure, and how the relationship amongst these experiences shapes our decision-making.

Thus far, we have addressed how the mind and body work together to seek out pleasurable experiences, to include a high-level understanding of how chemical changes in our body drive such behavior. Now we must spend some time exploring another critical attribute associated with the limbic system, and that is fear. Opposite of pleasure is fear, pain, or rejection. It is our human relationship with fear and how we are designed to cope with it that plays a major role in our ability to become a transcendent leader.

It is our primal behavior associated with fear that tends to dominate our minds and inhibit our ability to excel through effective communication. In the world of hierarchy and our inborn survival instincts, fear is central to how we communicate and cope with obstacles that interfere with our ability to move up the ladder or achieve acceptance. The primal instinct to survive, along with the social behaviors and communication challenges experienced along the way, must be recognized. It's the combination of these complexities that represents the greatest deterrent to effective leadership and your ability to sustain leadership transcendence.

This is why the idea of a perfect leader does not truly exist. The idea of becoming a perfect leader must be replaced with the idea of becoming a transcendent leader. Transcendent leaders are not perfect; however, they have accepted that they will never be perfect. Through a strong leadership foundation built by perpetual preparation, transcendent leaders recognize the inborn self-preservation that surrounds and inherently resides within them. There exists a constant battle that must be waged to ensure leadership transcendence prevails.

To better understand the internal conflicts that ensue, we must explore how our primal instincts, as they relate to fear, are instrumental in our ability to achieve leadership transcendence. When it comes to fear, our limbic system imposes a similar reaction as to when we experience pleasure. However, the process is different. The moment we start to feel fear, our brain's response system releases a chemical called corticotrophin (CRH) through the limbic portion of our brain. Once released, CRH initiates a stress response throughout the body that is made up of a sequence of events known as the hypothalamic-pituitary-adrenal axis (HPA). Through this reaction, the brain's response system begins to release another chemical called adrenocorticotrophic hormone (ACTH), which in turn causes the adrenal glands to release glucocorticoids, which are stress hormones such as cortisol (Schoen, 2013, p. 62) (Winston, 2002, p. 38).

These stress hormones enhance many of the body's biological reactions. This process impacts adrenal glands and initiates other adrenal hormones such as epinephrine and norepinephrine, which collectively activate the sympathetic nervous system. It is these collective events that activate your "fight," "flight," or "frozen" response system, which causes our body functions to change. We experience an increase in our blood pressure and heart rate.

As these reactions occur, something else of great significance begins. Our dopamine levels decrease. Similar to our experience as it relates to pleasure, we experience a change in our physical and emotional state of well-being. In the case of fear, as our dopamine levels decrease, we experience a negative or unpleasurable feeling. As with pleasure, neurons also collide in response to fear, thus creating a hardwired imprint in our brain that drives our instincts to avoid fear.

Opposite of pleasure, our reaction to fear compels the need to end the discomfort and fear as quickly as possible. It is through this compelling event that our brain hardwires this experience, thus helping to ensure we do not experience it again. Thereby, caring for our overall self-preservation, which we will come to recognize, often gets in the way of our ability to lead with transcendence.

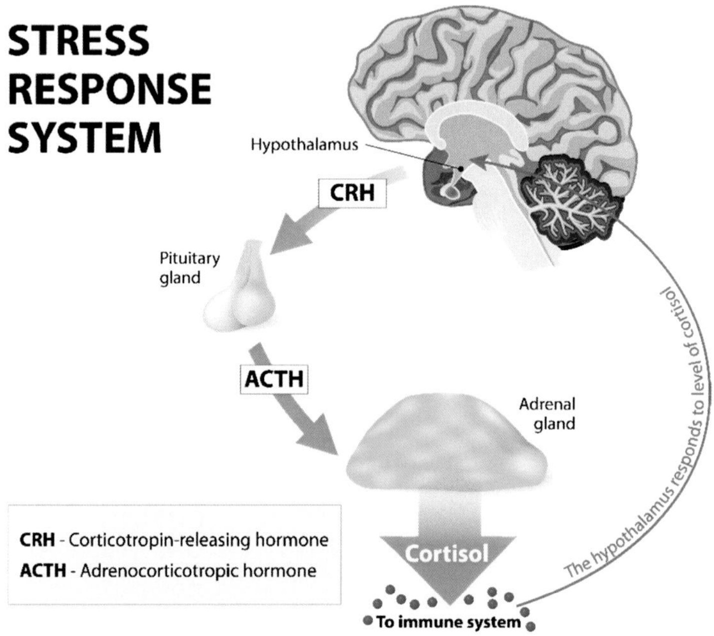

For example, studies have found that when asked what was more frightening, public speaking or being diagnosed with cancer, a majority of people would rather have cancer than speak in front of a large audience (Schoen, 2013). Certainly, when asked again, participants would likely change their answers. However, glossophobia, or speech anxiety associated with the fear of public speaking or of speaking in general, is abundant. An estimated 5.3 million Americans suffer from a social phobia, with 74 percent suffering from speech anxiety (Fadden, 2014). This is remarkable. What drives such bizarre behavior?

As we have learned, our bodies are predisposed through primal instincts to react to certain situations and events in a way that helps to ensure our overall self-preservation. Through our understanding of the brain and its fight-or-flight response, we can now understand how the fear of public speaking can invoke the fear of judgment, acceptance, or rejection. We can now understand how, through our survival instincts, our brain invokes a natural reaction through the limbic brain system that is predisposed to associate such fears as being in conflict with self-preservation. This, in return, initiates the subconscious survival instinct and chemical process that impacts and cements our response to both current and future events.

It is not uncommon for a leader to have public-speaking responsibilities, requiring them to present to both small and large audiences. We often marvel at those individuals, those with a perceived ability to speak to large audiences with little or no fear. The reality is we are all different, and yet in many ways we are all the same. Some of us have strengths, where others have weaknesses. Through a better understanding of what drives our fears, we are better able to apply cerebral analysis and thus allow ourselves the opportunity to grow, to learn the necessary skills to become better communicators and ultimately better leaders.

The complexities associated with the human brain play an intricate role in our ability to become better leaders and, in time, transcendent leaders. In fact, our brain is just like a computer. Similar to our neural networks and impulses (a.k.a.

computer bus), our brain incorporates such computer functions as data processing, memory caches, program applications, fast-processing power, and various two-way communications to a forever-engaging world. Like a computer, once we understand how all these components work together, we are better able to learn new skills and apply new programs that over time are intended to yield better, more consistent outcomes. Also like a computer, we are susceptible to viruses and bad behavior in the context of malware. Without this foundation, we run the risk of experiencing a nervous breakdown, or in computer terms, a blue screen.

To become a transcendent leader, you must recognize that similar to the advancement of computers, modern science has discovered the interrelationship between our physical and emotional primal behaviors. You must recognize the naturally occurring reactions within our brain in association with our self-preservation and survival instincts, and how these inter-relationships must be understood in order to establish and build upon a strong leadership foundation. In the case of hierarchy, it is our survival instincts and how our bodies react to certain situations that shape how we interact with those perceived to be in power.

These interactions and experiences shape who we are, our ambitions in life, our personalities, and our overall character. Just like a fingerprint, no two life experiences are exactly the same. It is through this dynamic that how we communicate and process what is being communicated determines the success of an overall human interaction. When you add to the challenge of such communication the inherent predisposed attributes associated with our survival instincts, it is easy to understand why becoming a transcendent leader is a process and not an event.

CHAPTER 3

PERSONALITY AND SELF-AWARENESS

If you talk to a man in a language he understands, that goes to his head. If you talk to him in his language, that goes to his heart.

—Nelson Mandela

Long before MRIs and modern science, attempts were made to better understand human interaction and the overall complexities inherent to effective communication based on personality and self-awareness. An individual who helped to pioneer and advance our understating of human interaction was Carl Gustav Jung. Jung was a well-known Swiss psychiatrist and psychotherapist who founded analytical psychology and contributed greatly to the science of personality theory. The central concept of analytical psychology is based on human individuation, a process of psychological integration. In Jung's *Collected Works*, Vol. 6, par. 757, Jung describes individuation as "the process by which individual beings are formed and differentiated [from other human beings]; in particular, it is the development of the psychological individual as a being distinct from the general, collective psychology" (C.G., 1971, p. 757). Through his work, Jung developed a foundational approach to the study of the human mind. Much of Jung's work and contributions focused on the unconscious mind and self-preservation. In *Psychological*

Types (The Collected Works of C.G. Jung, Vol. 6) he wrote, "I have been compelled, in my investigations into the structure of the unconscious, to make a conceptual distinction between soul and psyche. By psyche, I understand the totality of all psychic processes, conscious as well as unconscious. By soul, on the other hand, I understand a clearly demarcated functional complex that can best be described as a 'personality'" (C.G., 1971, p. 797).

Before we explore Jung's theory on personality, it is important to recognize that Jung was extremely aware of our human inborn instincts and the subconscious mind. As part of Jung's contribution to personality theory, his notion of the collective, or transpersonal, unconscious (Hidden You)—the relationship between our conscious and our unconscious innate instincts, which goes beyond personal identity—was his most controversial and original contribution of his time. Like many of the pioneers during their time, his thoughts and ideas were not accepted by many within the psychology community, as there was no scientific evidence to substantiate his theories. In an excerpt from *Personality and Personal Growth* (6th ed.) Frager, R., and Fadiman, J. state that "Jungian psychology focuses on establishing and fostering the relationship between conscious and unconscious processes" (Fager and Fadiman, 2005, p. 56). Dialogue between the conscious and the unconscious aspects of the psyche enriches the person, and Jung believed that without this understanding, unconscious processes can weaken and even jeopardize your personality. Jung believed strongly in a level of unconscious that comprised of past memories (instincts) from our ancestral and evolutionary past. In *Psychiatric Studies (The Collected Works of C.G. Jung Vol. 1.)*, Jung wrote, "The form of the world into which [a person] is born is already inborn in him, as a virtual image" (188). Jung had remarkable insight and intuition, considering that today's technology was not available during his time.

To uncover your Hidden You, we will leverage and explore Jung's contribution as it relates to personality types. Through his work, Carl Jung developed a theory of psychological types designed to categorize people in terms of various personality patterns. Jung's personality theory focused on four basic psychological functions: sensation, intuition, thinking, and feeling. Although Jung was a major contributor to the development and understanding of personality theory, it was his successors who took it to another level, making it more relevant to everyday life and society at large.

One of Jung's followers, and a significant contributor to the deeper understanding of our inherent human social-behavioral tendencies in relation to individual personality was Isabel Briggs Myers. In the 1940s, Isabel Briggs Myers began her research, and in 1982, shortly after her death, her book *Gifts Differing: Understanding Personality Type* was published (Myers, 1980). Her book was based on her life studies regarding human personality and reflected her extended interpretation of Carl Gustav Jung's personality types. Similar to Henry Alexander Murray, who we will explore in Chapter 5, Isabel was influenced by Jung's work regarding social behaviors and its relation to personality types. Isabel's goal in writing the book, while leveraging Jung's concepts, was to help ordinary people identify with the variations and complexities of personalities in the world. Thus, she emphasized "self-transcendence," helping others learn how to coexist and interact more successfully while dealing with the many challenges and social behaviors experienced throughout society. Isabel believed strongly that each person is born with different gifts, and through these inborn gifts, each of us has an inherent preference for how we use our minds, how we leverage our values, and how our feelings are invoked.

In researching Jung's work, Isabel further explored how Jung divided activities associated with human self-preservation into two simple mental activities. The first mental activity was associated with the consumption of new information and then achieving enhanced awareness through processing this new information. The second mental activity was the process of coming to a conclusion based on the awareness achieved through this new information. Where Jung's contribution to society was mostly related to personality types and his focus on helping those who suffered from mental illness, Isabel's focus and research was consumed in using Jung's discoveries to help ordinary and healthy people with understanding their personality type, and how personality type was commonly consumed and processed by others. Isabel recognized that how people process and respond to new information is not the same, and the inability to recognize these differences can create unnecessary stress and anxiety. She recognized that a common stress factor and deterrent toward effective communication was in the inability to recognize others' personality traits. Through her studies, she recognized how individuals are often baffled by the failure or inability of a recipient to understand and appreciate the logic of their position.

With great certainty, anyone reading this book has experienced at some point the inability to effectively communicate their desired logic or ideas. To be a transcendent leader, you must understand and embrace the psychological aspect of being a leader and the need to understand a follower's Hidden You in order to lead them to a successful outcome. You have to be able to adjust your Hidden You in order to effectively communicate, motivate, and inspire your followers toward achieving desired outcomes. Understanding personality types is a critical step toward building a strong leadership foundation. To build this foundation and continue the journey of identifying your Hidden You, we will explore Isabel Briggs Myers's remarkable work in greater detail through her expansion of Jung's theories and personality types.

The following sections are dedicated to laying the foundation for understanding your Hidden You. We will begin this process through Isabel Briggs Myers's contribution via the Myers-Briggs Type Indicator® (MBTI®) process. As you apply this to yourself, it is also important to recognize the attributes associated with those Hidden You personality traits that are not associated with your own. You must pay particular attention to those opposite or most different from your own. Transcendent leaders must understand their Hidden You, while also identifying the personality traits or Hidden You of others. Once you can clearly identify with your own traits, as well as those of others, you can increase your knowledge and understanding of how these traits can impact how you communicate with others.

Over many years, the MBTI has become a well-established, industry-recognized exercise for assessing individual personality type, and thus the reason it has been chosen as part of your leadership evolution. Before reading the next sections of this chapter, please visit www.myersbriggs.org to complete the MBTI. Once complete, please continue the reading. We will seek to more fully understand Isabel's defined process and descriptions in relation to your Hidden You.

BASIC TENETS OF MYERS-BRIGGS PERSONALITY TYPES

The purpose of the MBTI personality inventory is to make the theory of psychological personality types described by Jung more understandable and useful. The essence of the theory is that much of what feels random and complex in human social behavior is actually quite consistent and predictable. This observation, in large part, is due to the basic differences in the way individuals prefer to use their perception and overall judgment. Isabel stated, "Perception involves all the ways of becoming aware of things, people, happenings, or ideas. Judgment involves all the ways of coming to conclusions about what has been perceived. If people differ systematically in what they perceive and in how they reach conclusions, then it is only reasonable for them to differ correspondingly in their interests, reactions, values, motivations, and skills" (Myers, 1980).

In developing the MBTI, the aim of Isabel, with help from her mother, Katharine Briggs, was to make the insights of personality-type theory more accessible to individuals and groups. In support of this effort, Isabel addressed two related goals in the development and application of the MBTI.

In association with their unique differences, the first goal was the identification of basic preferences of each of the four psychological types (sensation, intuition, thinking, and feeling) specified or implicit in Jung's theory. The second goal was the creation, identification, and description of the sixteen distinctive personality types that Isabel believed resonated from the interactions among the basic preferences. Through the creation of the MBTI types, Isabel created and expanded Jung's basic preferences into a dynamic and complex interrelated system. Through this process, she facilitated the creation and identification of the different components of a person's psychological makeup that interrelated in such a way to establish both balance and effectiveness. In doing so, Isabel concluded that your actual personality type is a lifelong developmental process, where many factors can affect the direction of its development, as well as type variances over a lifetime.

Within the basic tenets of Myers-Briggs personality types, and using your MBTI results, the first and last letters in your personality-type results are called attitudes, or orientations, because they have to do with how you interact with the world. The middle two letters are called your mental functions, because they are the basis for much of your brain's work. The two sets together are called your function pair.

The Attitudes (Orientations)

Within the MBTI types there are four attitudes (or orientations) that reflect the ways you are energized and how you structure, or live, your life. The first two are ***Extraversion*** and ***Introversion.***

According to Jung, Extraversion and Introversion are complementary attitudes (or orientations) of energy (Myers I. B., 2003). Those who prefer ***Extraversion*** tend to direct energy outward and are energized by the outside world. Those who prefer ***Introversion*** tend to direct energy inward and are energized by reflecting on their inner world. Not as defined within both Jung's and Myers's work is the inborn association with fear and self-preservation. However, as we explore these orientations, do recognize the inherent interrelationship between self-preservation and how the orientations may be impacted by conscious and subconscious survival instincts.

The other two attitudes (or orientations) are ***Judging*** and ***Perceiving. Judging*** and ***Perceiving,*** while implied in Jung's work, were constructed by Isabel Briggs Myers to further refine the applications of psychological type. People who prefer the ***Judging*** attitude are likely to come to conclusions quickly and enjoy the structure provided by reaching closure. People who prefer the ***Perceiving*** attitude are likely to take more time to gather information before comfortably coming to closure. They enjoy the process, and are more comfortable being open-ended.

To gain an additional perspective, the following is excerpted from the *MBTI Manual: A Guide to the Development and Use of the Myers-Briggs Type Indicator* (Myers I. B., 2003).

- **Favorite world:** Do you prefer to focus on the outer world or on your own inner world? This is called ***Extraversion (E)*** or ***Introversion (I)***.
- **Structure:** In dealing with the outside world, do you prefer to get things decided, or do you prefer to stay open to new information and options? This is called ***Judging (J)*** or ***Perceiving (P)***.

The Mental Functions

Within the MBTI type are four mental functions: ***Sensing, Intuition, Thinking,*** and ***Feeling.*** Everyone has and uses all four functions, even though only two of them are part of your MBTI personality type. In fact, you probably couldn't get through the day or life as we know it without using all of them in some form or fashion.

The first two mental functions are for gathering information and are used for perception. The first is ***Sensing (S). Sensing (S)*** perception pays attention to details and current realities. The second perception mental function is ***Intuition (N). Intuition (N)*** perception pays attention to meanings, patterns, and future possibilities.

The next two mental functions are for organizing information and making judgments. The first is ***Thinking (T). Thinking (T)*** chooses decisions based on principles and logical consequences. The second is ***Feeling (F). Feeling (F)*** chooses decisions based on values and consequences for people.

To gain an additional perspective of the MBTI-type mental functions, the following is excerpted from the *MBTI Manual: A Guide to the Development and Use of the Myers-Briggs Type Indicator* (Myers I. B., 2003).

- **Information:** Do you prefer to focus on the basic information you take in, or do you prefer to interpret and add meaning? This is called ***Sensing (S)*** or ***Intuition (N).***
- **Decisions:** When making decisions, do you prefer to first look at logic and consistency, or first look at the people and special circumstances? This is called ***Thinking (T)*** or ***Feeling (F).***

Although everyone has access to and uses all four mental functions, each personality type prefers to use these functions in an order best suited to their needs. In personality-type theory, the preferred order of these functions is considered to be instinctive (your Hidden You). Keep in mind that the order can be changed when circumstances require you to make decisions or solve problems in an alternative manner.

Using your MBTI results, you can now evaluate your personality based on your four-letter code. In total, there are sixteen different MBTI personality types. The sheer volume of personality types is confirmation of the inborn complexities inherent to each of us, and represents another confirmation for why perpetual preparation is essential to bettering our odds of hitting a transcendent leadership hole-in-one. To achieve leadership transcendence, it is worthwhile to spend some time to understand the nature of each personality type. The next section of this chapter will highlight the sixteen personality types of the MBTI. As you explore each personality type, reflect on how each type corresponds to your own. Recognize that the personality types opposite yours are where you will want to spend some extra time exploring. As part of your leadership evolution, you will come to recognize that the majority of your communication challenges and inability to connect with others will be associated with those individuals who are most opposite of your MBTI personality.

More in-depth descriptions of the sixteen personality types can be found at www.myersbriggs.org. The following is a condensed version of each type:

ISTJ - Quietly systematic. Factual. Organized. Logical. Detailed.
ISTP - Logical. Quietly analytical. Practical. Adaptable.
ISFJ - Quietly warm. Factual. Sympathetic. Detailed.
ISFP - Gentle. Quietly caring. Compassionate. Adaptable.
INFJ - Vision and meaning oriented. Quietly intense. Insightful. Creative.

INFP - Deep-felt valuing. Quietly caring. Compassionate. Pursues meaning.
INTJ - Vision oriented. Quietly innovative. Insightful. Conceptual.
INTP - Logical. Conceptual. Analytical. Objective.
ESTJ - Active organizer. Logical. Assertive. Fact minded.
ESTP - Excitement seeking. Active. Pragmatic. Direct.
ESFJ - Actively sociable. Warm. Harmonizer. Caring.
ESFP - Energetic. Sociable. Practical. Friendly.
ENFJ - Actively sociable. Enthusiastic. Harmonizer. Expressive.
ENFP - Enthusiastic. Imaginative. Energetic. Creative.
ENTJ - Driving organizer. Planner. Vision focused. Decisive.
ENTP - Energetic. Inventive. Enthusiastic. Abstract.

Understanding and identifying your personality type is required throughout your lifetime, and can vary based on circumstance. Through our new understanding of our inborn primitive survival instincts, and how our brain contributes to the process of pleasure, fear, and anxiety, we can better understand our unique personality-type tendencies and their relationship to self-preservation. Through these tendencies, you can reflect on past experiences, and use those past experiences to better understand how this new knowledge could have benefited the overall communication and interaction required to ensure and drive an intended outcome.

CHAPTER 4

LEADERSHIP GENETICS

Before you are a leader success is all about growing yourself. When you become a leader success is all about growing others.

—Jack Welch

When it comes to leadership, there are different views as to whether someone is born with inherent qualities and attributes associated with being able to lead. Some might say you either have it or you don't. My personal belief is that anyone can learn how to be an effective and transcendent leader. To do so with transcendence, you must first come to understand your Hidden You and identify your subconscious strengths and weaknesses.

Within every Hidden You are blind spots, or weaknesses, that will hinder the ability to be recognized as a leader, denying the opportunity to reach leadership transcendence. There are individuals who have strengths or existing leadership attributes within their Hidden You personalities that drive the perception of innate or inborn leadership qualities, thus enabling a more direct path toward leadership opportunity, even when that individual is not truly ready or qualified to lead. In contrast, through knowledge of Hidden You and in support of those who may lack perceived innate or inborn leadership qualities, where weaknesses in personality are in conflict with group dynamics, they too can obtain leadership opportunity and eventual leadership transcendence. Through blind-spot recognition, in conjunction with "move" and "adapt" concepts, you will be able to better understand why these weaknesses occur and perhaps better understand their origin.

Beyond the MBTI® and the sixteen different personality traits, there exists a deeper, more rooted aspect of who we are as individuals, and how we receive and interact within the world around us. Just as I took on the golf attributes of my father, I also took on a resemblance of my family system. Whether it was my father, mother, sister, or close family acquaintances, they each had an impact and played a role in shaping my Hidden You. They each contributed to how I dealt with success or failure. Additionally, my family system would influence how I would perceive and react to my own inborn survival instincts.

Through my own leadership evolution, and my Hidden You self-evaluation, there have been internal observations and experiences that upon reflection were not 100 percent attributable to just my personality trait as defined by MBTI. An added dimension existed, a dimension that also incorporated inherent traits associated with overall character, trustworthiness, and moral strength, and how these attributes resonated when having to interact with those of authority (hierarchy) or in power (power not limited to career progression but to those in control of a circumstance or desired outcome, to include our overall well-being). Early in my career, I discovered that when around those in power, my physiological and psychological demeanor would change. My subconscious, inborn survival instinct would provoke internal physiological fear. Within me there existed a dimension that dealt with some foreign emotion and response to both adverse and even euphoric situations when having to intermingle or interact with those in power. How you instinctively react to such circumstances when dealing with those in power is essential to understanding the Hidden You, and is often a direct reflection that provides good insight into how our family system influenced our behavior.

During my time in college, well before I had even understood the importance of leadership evolution and the need for perpetual preparation, the local YMCA blessed me with the opportunity to run a teen camp program. As part of the program, I was managing four camp counselors and forty-plus teenagers. Upon reflection, running a teen summer-camp program in many ways was far more challenging than running a P&L or leading grown-up adults. Remarkably, the same social behaviors and interrelational group dynamics that occurred back then still occur today: parents not relating to their kids due to lack of communication or broken homes; camp counselors making bad decisions and having to learn how to effectively communicate root cause and subsequent plan of action to get back on course and regain good standing; unexpected events, and having to communicate to a group of parents with a multitude of personality types and learning styles that need to be confronted to ensure they understand the situation, and that their child is safe and in good hands.

As Jung and Isabel discovered, how individuals consume information, regardless of age, and the inherent preference for how we use our minds, values, and feelings exist throughout our lifetime. Running a teen camp at the local YMCA provided a front-row seat for how our personal upbringing and family system has conditioned our instincts and our response to society's events and circumstance. This includes situations that require communication extended to those with power.

These situations are consumed by an observation of power and hierarchy of who is in control. As individuals, we are most comfortable and happy when we feel like we're in control, or that when being led, our leader is facilitating an environment in which we are contributing to the desired outcome or greater purpose. How an individual interprets being led, or how they interpret the process for leading others is often not dictated by logic, but instinctively developed and influenced by outside influences such as our family system.

I observed this throughout my early leadership evolution, yet I did not fully understand it until my perpetual-preparation activities led me to read *Power Genes: Understanding your Power Persona—and How to Wield It at Work* by Maggie Craddock (Craddock, 2011). Through Craddock's unique experiences as an executive coach, she articulates how personality traits in association with power personas (different styles of exerting influence) can influence or jeopardize your ability to advance within an organization or company. Maggie discovered that many of the reactions individuals have within or outside of the job stem from self-preservation instincts when associating with those in power. The type of reactions that can cause someone to come across as either a dictator or a subservient bystander are often rooted in behaviors internalized or experienced when interacting within their family system. As a newborn, from the time we are able to reason, the need for self-preservation and our interactions with those who meet our needs, our family system, play a significant role in influencing and shaping who we are.

The human instinct of self-preservation is central to who we are and how we socially interact with others. Both consciously and subconsciously, it is our instinctive self-preservation that often determines our success or failure as transcendent leaders. In the attempt to better understand social behaviors, studies have shown how self-preservation is built into our survival instincts.

One study, conducted on infants, provided insight into how preverbal infants make judgments based on observed social behaviors (Hamlin, November 2007). In this study, infants observed a "climber" in the form of a round disk of wood with large eyes glued onto its "face." The "climber" would start at the bottom of a hill and repeatedly attempt to reach the top of the hill. As part of the study, the "climber" would continuously fail to make the journey. After several failed attempts, a "helper" in the form of a triangle with similar big eyes would sometimes approach from below the "climber," helping to push the climber to the top. Also as part of the study, alternatively, a "hinderer" in the form of a square with big eyes would sometimes approach the "climber" from above and shove the "climber" back down the hill.

The objective of this study was to determine if the infants, after observing the aforementioned scenario over several iterations, would react to the "climber," "helper," or "hinderer" as appealing or aversive. In the same way an infant can display or show displeasure when presented with a certain food or toy, each character was presented back to the infant to determine how they would react. The result was that the infant would demonstrate a definite reluctance or unwillingness to reach for the "hinderer" as compared to the "helper."

To further the study, the infants observed additional scenarios. For example, in one scenario the "climber" was encountered by a "helper" and a "neutral" character who would do nothing. In another scenario, a "hinderer" and a "neutral" character were observed. The study found that the infants overwhelmingly preferred the "helper" to the "neutral," and they preferred the "neutral" to the "hinderer."

The results of the study were significant, as the findings showed that even six-month-old infants consider an individual's actions toward others when determining whether those actions are appealing, aversive, or self-preserving. The overall findings of the study provided evidence that preverbal infants assess individuals based on their behavior toward others.

This study is a good example of how the conscious and subconscious minds work together to formulate a social behavior that can be attributed to self-preservation. We can conclude that from the time we are able to observe interactions and events that surround us, even as infants, we are predisposed as part of our subconscious survival instinct to apply a form of social evaluation that is the foundation for our moral compass and actions toward others. More importantly, as infants we are naturally attracted to those elements that serve our self-preservation and survival, while we repel the unkind or those unwilling to help. This form of social evaluation is both subconsciously and, over time, consciously applied to all human interaction and is a critical element to how we connect with others. It is through this social-evaluation process, our experiences (both good and bad), and our built-in survival instincts that we build our own internal perceptions and our own reality when interacting with others.

Through a deeper understanding of your power persona, developed over time through the family system, you will be better prepared to know when to leverage or bypass an inherent power persona to be a more successful and effective leader. When it comes to being a transcendent leader, it is important to recognize that the majority of challenges experienced in business or in association with family matters are often a result of our own internal conflicts and our interpretation of what or who is in conflict with our self-preservation. As part of your leadership evolution, by learning and understanding how your upbringing or family system has influenced the personality-style differences between yourself and others, it will facilitate an ability to recognize and adapt to situations that involve those with whom you lead and with those with whom you follow. Maggie Craddock summed it up perfectly: "You don't just want to focus on how you're coming across, you want to focus on how other people feel about themselves in your presence" (Stillman, 2011).

Understanding your relationship to authority and your relationship to others when in authority helps you understand your effect on others. To help determine this, Maggie Craddock developed what she calls the "Power Grid," which identifies four power-persona types. As part of your leadership evolution, and to further define your Hidden You, you need to identify which power persona you dominate. This is accomplished by examining your dominant emotional triggers and behavioral patterns. Most individuals find that their overall power persona is a blend of at least two of the four core power personas.

Maggie Craddock published an article in the *Harvard Business Review* on May 9, 2011, called "What's Your Power Style?" In the article, Maggie highlights the four power-persona styles as follows:

THE PLEASER

Due to outside stressors, Pleasers often didn't get the attention they craved from their caretakers early in life. Pleasers often grow up hungry for validation and are hardwired to take care of others. Pleasers often wield power by attempting to connect with others at a personal level.

THE CHARMER

Charmers were often required to soothe an emotionally needy parent early in life. As a result, they sometimes have little respect for formal authority and may manipulate others in order to get their needs met. The Charmer power style is exemplified by people with an intensity of focus that both intimidates and seduces others into compliance.

THE INSPIRER

The family systems that foster Inspirers often value self-expression over conformity, and the caregivers in such systems are often willing to make personal sacrifices to achieve excellence in areas such as artistic expression or scientific inquiry. Inspirers tend to be innovative thinkers and operate with a consistent commitment to the greater good.

THE COMMANDER

Often, a Commander has grown up in a family system devoted to sports, religion, the military, or any larger system that reinforces discipline and a strict code of conduct. Commanders operate with a results orientation and tend to foster a sense of urgency in others.

With a solid foundation of Hidden You personality-type analysis, through the lens of these power personas, your Hidden You will continue to take shape, better preparing you to identify with others in a more systematic approach. With this knowledge, your ability to engage through leadership transcendence goes up exponentially.

It was through this knowledge that I observed a trend throughout society and at work today. I discovered and observed that it was not uncommon for leaders and managers without Hidden You insight or analysis to align themselves with like-minded personalities. On the surface, this may not seem major. However, to be an effective leader or manager, it is important to surround yourself with different personalities and power personas to ensure you are exposed to different perspectives and ideas.

Early in my career, I performed the Myers-Briggs Personality Indicator assessment test with my team. Having just completed the test for myself, I felt the urge to better understand the personality traits of each individual on my team. The results were astounding. It was through this process that I discovered the common phenomenon of leaders surrounding themselves with like-minded individuals or those with similar personalities. My Myers-Briggs personality is INTJ, which is uncommon. Out of the fifteen people I was managing at the time, four members of my team had the exact same personality. It is important to point out that of these four individuals, I did not inherit any of them; I interviewed and hired all of them onto my team. It is my belief and observation that this same phenomenon is happening throughout the business world today.

Based on your power persona, and the nature of its dominant characteristics, this tendency can have unintended consequences. In today's society, with less focus on building healthy cultures and healthy working environments and more focus on the bottom line, it is logical to assume there would be an increase in Commander power personas getting promoted into leadership and managerial roles. The high stakes and need for instant financial gratification complements the power persona of a Commando, essentially forming a perfect union.

This observation is not an indictment on those who have a dominant Commander power persona. Without question, leaders and managers with this persona have had and continue to have successful careers, yielding significant contributions to the workplace and society at large. However, as is the case for all Myers-Briggs personalities and Maggie's power personas, if a leader or manager has not begun their leadership evolution and lacks the critical knowledge of their inherent attributes, they will struggle with their inborn self-preservation, limiting their ability to connect with other power personas. For example, it is highly likely that those with a non-Commander power persona who are being led by a Commander power persona will find it difficult to work for such a leader. Due to the dominant power persona of the Commander, whose innate self-preservation drives an instinctively competitive and results-oriented persona, it is not uncommon to observe a leader or manager with this power persona experiencing low moral or unhealthy culture amongst their team or organization.

The book *The No Asshole Rule,* written by Robert I. Sutton, is one of my favorite all-time books. The title alone should be enough to pique the interest of anyone who has ever worked in a difficult environment or for a difficult boss. Upon reading the book, I concluded that the book was mostly written in response to the many Commander personas who have not begun their individual Hidden You analysis. In *The No Asshole Rule,* Robert says he wrote the book "because there is so much evidence that civilized workplaces are not a naïve dream, that they do exist, and that pervasive contempt can be erased and replaced with mutual respect when a team or organization is managed right—and civilized workplaces usually enjoy superior performance as well" (Sutton, 2007).

Another important component to Maggie's Power Genes personality theory is her creation of the Power Grid. The Power Grid facilitates how to diagnose your power persona. More importantly, once understood, Maggie identifies common strengths as well as common destructive behaviors, or what she calls "blind spots," often projected and associated with an identified power persona. Based on the traits associated with the less-dominant power genes within the Power Grid, Maggie provides tremendous insight into how to more effectively interact with individual peers, bosses, or even family who connect via different dominant power personas.

Putting Maggie's recommendations to the test, and at the time of reading her book, I was being led by a strong Commander persona. Early in my career I had the brief opportunity to create a dialog regarding leadership and management with this individual. I asked if they could suggest any good books or seminars regarding leadership and management. The answer was certainly interesting, as the response was a definitive "Don't know of any, and it is a waste of time."

Over the course of many years, and through multiple organizational changes, it was a true blessing to have been given the opportunity to work for this individual. We had a wonderful personal relationship, and regardless of our power-persona conflict, I would certainly go out of my way to support anything this individual ever asked for or needed. It was through this relationship and opportunity that my own leadership evolution continued to grow. As my understanding of the Hidden You became clearer, my ability to "move" and "adapt" to the various personalities and power personas facilitated my ability to be a more effective communicator. To better understand the realities of human social behaviors and the Hidden You, I put this new knowledge to the test.

Leveraging the existing relationship and inherent Commander power persona of my leader at the time, I wanted to observe how adapting to his Hidden You would impact our ability to connect. Over time, I observed that this leader demonstrated a strong tendency to limit creative thinking and the sharing of alternative approaches. The focus was more about getting from Point A to Point B, and the road map to get there was provided by this individual. This leader had all the answers, and once their mind was set, there was no changing it.

In direct contrast, and in association with my dominant Pleaser persona, our power personas were directly opposite on the Power Grid. So one day, as part of a personal experiment, I decided that for two weeks, I would agree with everything my Commando leader communicated. I would adjust my communication to reflect the Commander power persona—a task I would find easier said than done. At the end of the first two weeks, the results were remarkable. I was amazed at just how well we got along. It was as if the stars had aligned and the sky had opened the doorway to heaven. Looking back, it was the best we had ever interacted at work, and I felt more appreciated than ever.

Of course, that was until I went back to my normal Pleaser self, to include my Myers-Briggs Personality Indicator of INTJ (introversion, intuition, thinking, judgment), a vision-oriented personality who is quietly innovative and insightful. An INTJ is not innately comfortable with being given a road map to follow without first having the opportunity to contribute.

If I had to guess, my Commando leader was more like an ESTJ—an active organizer who is logical, assertive, and results oriented. This is as close to my opposite as you can get. All in all, the experiment was a tremendous eye-opener and a critical step in understanding the importance of the Hidden You.

From that day forward, the significance of understanding different personalities and their impact on a leader's success or failure was self-evident. It also opened my eyes to the overall impact the Hidden You has on social behaviors and group dynamics. Through recognizing our inborn survival instincts and our innate desire to find acceptance, we can begin to understand the complexities of human communication.

CHAPTER 5

LEADERSHIP PSYCHOLOGY

I can calculate the motion of heavenly bodies, but not the madness of people.

—Isaac Newton

With a solid understanding of your Hidden You now taking shape, we can now explore how social behaviors and group dynamics impact your ability to lead transcendentally through social and situational awareness. To do this, we will explore the basic tenets of social behaviors and group dynamics. With a fundamental understanding of leadership psychology, you can better understand how your Hidden You impacts such behaviors and how they are applied to associated group dynamics. It is through this concept that we will also explore followership transcendence.

First, with the knowledge of the human brain and recognition of how primal survival instincts impact how we react to the world around us, we also need to identify and understand how our Hidden You impacts social behaviors that facilitate our ability to connect as individuals and within groups. As a transcendent leader, you must relate to both an individual and a group. It is through the combination of our survival instincts and social behaviors that individuals and groups form a perception of reality. When it comes to leadership transcendence, it is important to understand how social behaviors can influence an individual's perception of situations and circumstances, and how a group of individuals can sway and influence this individual's perception of reality. This applies even when these views and perceptions are not in everyone's best interest.

When it comes to individuals and groups, social behaviors that have a direct lineage to our primitive brain, like the need for group acceptance, play a major role in how our subconscious survival instincts can distort our perception of reality. To become a transcendent leader, you must understand how social behaviors in relation to those in power, or hierarchy, have conscious and subconscious control over those of less power, and how this relationship of power and hierarchy can distort the views of reality, where reality is manipulated to yield an outcome that is more favorable for a select few than the collective whole. This element of power and hierarchy is found in all species, and is central to how social behaviors impact the need for social acceptance. In our society, there exists an element of hierarchy which is most often associated with the need for power or sense of control. Humans have an innate desire, some greater than others, to feel in control. It is important to recognize that control does not always translate to power, and power does not always translate to leadership transcendence. As humans, we gravitate toward areas of comfort to reduce our fears and anxieties, and toward situations and environments that cater to our primitive survival instinct and need for self-preservation.

From the time we are born, our need to connect with others is already present. Our capacity to connect, evaluate others, and navigate the social world is essential to our overall self-preservation. Socially, we must be able to make good decisions based on the actions and intentions of those we connect and communicate with.

In the process of connecting and interacting through various forms of communication, we make decisions regarding who we should consider a friend or a threat. We are often required to use our conscious and subconscious minds to rapidly evaluate people on the basis of both behavioral and physical features. This ability begins early in life and continues throughout your lifetime. With each observation and experience, as described in Chapter 2, events are hardwired into our brains.

To be a transcendent leader, you must explore and understand the interdependencies of how our social-evaluation process—our evaluation of others' intentions—in conjunction with our Hidden You guides our inborn need for acceptance. Through this innate desire to belong, as individuals, we are better equipped to deal with the many challenges that subconsciously threaten our inborn survival and self-preservation.

It is the primitive instinct and struggle for acceptance that drives the critical need to obtain a foundational understanding of leadership psychology. Leadership psychology is important, as it emphasizes the need to understand individual and group behaviors as a complex system in order to achieve positive and long-lasting change (Wikipedia, n.d.). Additionally, it integrates the study and practice of leadership and organizational systems with the fundamentals of human psychology to establish a new generation of thinking and approach to leadership. It is through the correlation of the thoughts, feelings, and social behaviors associated with leadership psychology that we can understand the enormity and complexity of the human spirit, the importance of perpetual preparation, and the need for a systematic approach to better the odds of leading transcendentally.

To begin our foundational understanding of leadership psychology and the social behaviors that guide us, we will begin with Abraham Maslow's hierarchy of needs, which describes the patterns of motivation that humans traverse. Just like our desire for "things," our self-preservation and motivational needs drive our social behavior and subsequent interaction with others. In his 1943 paper "A Theory of Human Motivation," published in the *Psychological Review*, Maslow describes the stages of growth in humans. Coining the terms "physiological," "safety," "belongingness" and "love," "esteem," "self-actualization," and "self-transcendence" as part of his needs theory, Maslow described the pattern or sequence by which human motivations generally evolve.

In his 1954 book *Motivation and Personality*, Maslow describes his hierarchy of needs theory, which today is commonly portrayed in the shape of a pyramid. The largest, most fundamental levels reside at the bottom of the pyramid, and the need for self-actualization resides at the top. Using this theory, we can better understand what drives our social behaviors based on how our inherent needs are being met (Maslow, 1954). The most fundamental and basic four layers of Maslow's pyramid (starting at the bottom) consist of what he refers to as "deficiency needs" or "D-needs." Deficiency needs, as articulated by Maslow, consist of esteem, friendship and love, security, and physical needs. Maslow theorized that all deficiency needs have a direct influence on our social behaviors with others. If a deficiency need is not being met, with the exception of the most fundamental physical need, then an individual will feel anxious and tense. Maslow's theory suggests that the most basic level of needs must be accounted for before an individual will intuitively seek out the secondary or higher-level needs, as depicted within the pyramid.

Maslow described physiological needs as the physical requirements for human survival, representing the first need we require. If any of these needs are not met, the human body cannot function properly and will ultimately fail. Physiological needs consist of air, water, and food. Secondary physiological needs would be clothing and shelter, which provide protection from harsh elements.

In the absence of physiological needs, Maslow's theory assumes that the need for safety takes precedence. Safety would consist of human behavior associated with ensuring personal security, financial security, health, and overall well-being. After physiological and safety needs are met, the third level of human needs are interpersonal, which involve feelings of belonging. It is within this third layer that Maslow acknowledges the impact of social-behavior deficiencies or disruption. In the context of the Hidden You, these are blind spots—personality and power personas in conflict with others—that within Maslow's hierarchy can adversely affect an individual's ability to form and maintain emotionally significant relationships in society.

According to Maslow, humans have an instinctive need to belong. In today's society, these social groups can be made up of the family system to include friends and coworkers. In addition, other social groups might consist of social clubs, religious groups, professional organizations, sports teams, and in extreme cases, groups focused on illegal crime.

Maslow's theory contends that humans need to love and be loved (Maslow A. H., 1943). They need to belong; they need acceptance. Love can be both sexual and nonsexual. When a connection or sense of belonging ceases to exist, many people are overwhelmed by loneliness, which often leads to social anxiety and depression. Thus, achieving acceptance within group dynamics is essential to caring for your self-preservation.

In Maslow's *Theory of Human Motivation,* he expands upon his needs theory by incorporating the need for esteem. He contends that all humans have a need to feel respected, and have an instinctive need for both self-respect and overall self-esteem. According to this theory, esteem represents the common human desire to be accepted and to be valued by others. Individuals will often seek out groups amongst their profession or hobbies to feel a sense of belonging and acceptance through contribution and perceived value or purpose. Without this type of interaction, it is not uncommon for low self-esteem to develop, and like loneliness, it often leads to depression.

Without a sense of acceptance or belonging, individuals often lose their sense of hierarchy or purpose in a group. As a result, individuals with low self-esteem often counter the associated emotions by consciously and subconsciously seeking attention to gain or regain group respect. Counterintuitively, this common reaction or social behavior does not help obtain the high self-esteem they wish to achieve, at least not until they are able to truly identify with their Hidden You.

Once esteem needs are met, Maslow describes an individual graduating to what he termed as the need for "self-actualization." Maslow describes this level as the desire to accomplish everything possible, "to become everything that one is capable of becoming" (Maslow A. H., *Motivation and Personality*, 1987, p. 22). Maslow states, "What humans can be, they must be" (Maslow A. H., *Motivation and Personality*, 1987, p. 22). The self-actualization need is about an individual recognizing their full potential. Through this recognition, the individual will often dedicate their focus and time within the context of their specific need. For example, one individual may have the strong desire to become a recognized international piano player. Another example would be the desire to achieve respect and admiration in the context of sports.

Toward the end of Maslow's career, he incorporated another need into his hierarchy called "self-transcendence." Through continued observations and study, Maslow believed that an individual only finds true self-transcendence upon surrendering to some higher purpose or goal. In other words, it's not about their self-preservation; it is about leveraging the skills they have mastered to ensure the self-preservation of others. Thus, a representation of the highest level in leadership: leadership transcendence.

MASLOW's HIERARCHY OF NEEDS

Self-actualization

This level of need refers to what a person's full potential is and the realization of that potential. Maslow describes this level as the desire to accomplish everything that one can, to become the most that one can be. Individuals may perceive or focus on this need very specifically. For example, one individual may have the strong desire to become an ideal parent. In another, the desire may be expressed athletically. For others, it may be expressed in paintings, pictures, or inventions.

Esteem

All humans have a need to feel respected; this includes the need to have self-esteem and self-respect. Esteem presents the typical human desire to be accepted and valued by others. People often engage in a profession or hobby to gain recognition.
These activities give the person a sense of contribution or value. Low self-esteem or an inferiority complex may result from imbalances during this level in the hierarchy.

RATIONAL BRAIN

INTERMEDIATE BRAIN

Self actualization

Esteem

Love, Belonging

Safety

Physiological

INTERMEDIATE BRAIN

PRIMITIVE BRAIN

PRIMITIVE BRAIN

Love and belonging

After physiological and safety needs are fulfilled, the third level of human needs is interpersonal and involves feelings of belongingness. This need is especially strong in childhood and can override the need for safety as witnessed in children who cling to abusive parents.

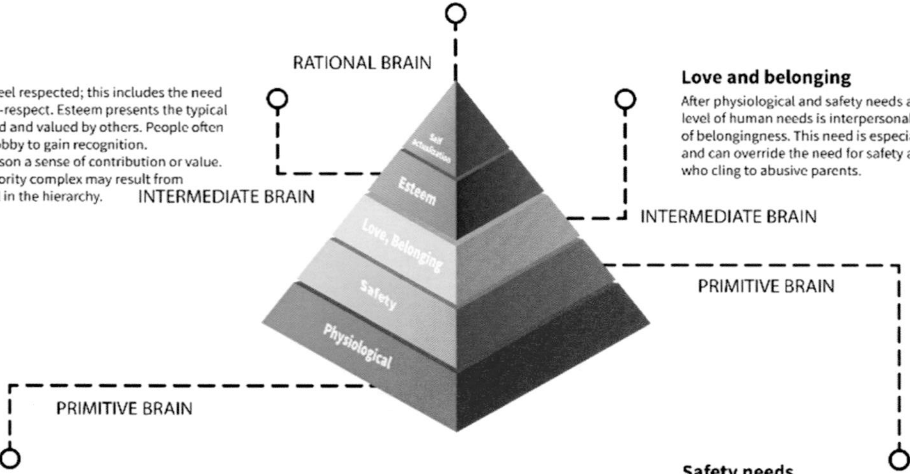

Physiological need

Physiological needs are the physical requirements for human survival. If these requirements are not met, the human body cannot function properly and will ultimately fail. Physiological needs are thought to be the most important; they should be met first.

Safety needs

With their physical needs relatively satisfied, the individual's safety needs take precedence and dominate behavior. In the absence of physical safety – due to war, natural disaster, family violence, childhood abuse, etc. – people may (re-)experience post-traumatic stress disorder or transgenerational trauma. This level is more likely to be found in children because they generally have a greater need to feel safe.

A good example of "self-transcendence" is Tim Tebow, former starting quarterback for the University of Florida. Tim, the winner of the most prestigious award in college football, the college football Heisman Trophy, was not able to fulfill his desire to have a lasting career in the National Football League. However, throughout his life and as part of his family system, he has been an active participant in helping others accept faith through the spiritual recognition of Jesus Christ. Tim Tebow grew up the son of missionaries, where for most of his life he participated in the missionary cause that his father and mother established in the Philippines. Early in his life and beyond his time at the University of Florida, Tim devoted himself to helping others. He sacrificed a great deal of personal time with a laser focus on raising money for pediatric cancer patients and disadvantaged children. In 2010, he started the Tim Tebow Foundation to bring faith, hope, and love to those needing a brighter day in their darkest hour of need (Tebow, 2016).

Through Tim's family system and perpetual preparation in his spiritual cause, Tim mastered the needs of Maslow's "physiological," "safety," "belongingness" and "love," "esteem," and "self-actualization" at an early age. Through Tim's own discovery of his Hidden You, he has now reached the highest level of Maslow's needs theory of "self-transcendence." Tim has found true self-transcendence through surrendering himself to a higher purpose, where his focus is not on his self-preservation, but on that of others. Through Tim Tebow's many endeavors, he has become a true representation of leadership transcendence.

What stands out among Maslow's work versus other psychologists was his ability to study what he called exemplary people, individuals such as Albert Einstein, Jane Addams, Eleanor Roosevelt, and Frederick Douglass. Unlike many psychologists, some of whom we will explore later in this chapter, rather than focusing on the mentally ill, Maslow studied the healthiest among us. Maslow believed that "the study of crippled, stunted, immature, and unhealthy specimens can yield only a crippled psychology and a crippled philosophy" (Maslow A. H., *Motivation and Personality*, 1954, p. 236). I suspect Maslow's interest in this field was driven in large part by the fact that he was diagnosed as "mentally unstable" at a young age. Using his own theory, in many ways, Maslow's self-actualization and then self-transcendence is a reflection of his own self-preservation and for the self-preservation of others.

Through Maslow's theories, we can adapt and influence positive, more effective social behaviors by having a clear understanding of our Hidden You. Influencing adaptive change rather than superficial change is an important characteristic of leadership transcendence. Transcendent leaders are able to influence positive change by being authentic, humble, and with a desire to adapt to others. Change through leadership transcendence requires social and situational awareness, and an innate desire to accommodate the self-preservation of all. Social and situational awareness allows you to adapt an interaction in a way that accounts for and neutralizes your bias toward others.

To achieve effective social and situational awareness, you must know how social behaviors and group dynamics drive different patterns and bias, both consciously and subconsciously, when leading others or when being led. To demonstrate, we will need to explore social evaluation processes associated with psychology attributes, such as the implicit personality theory and the covariation model.

The implicit personality theory is a form of social evaluation that describes the specific patterns and biases an individual uses when forming impressions or opinions of another person without having enough information or having had a sufficient amount of interaction with that person (Pendersen, 1965). Have you ever been with an acquaintance you trust, and upon meeting someone for the first time, one of you turns to the other and states something like, "That person is weird" or "For some reason, I don't trust that person"?

While there are components of the social evaluation process that are situational, as part of the implicit personality theory, individuals are still apt to form impressions and opinions across a variety of different circumstances based on their Hidden You tendencies and their subconscious or conscious need for self-preservation and acceptance (Cronbach, 1955). For example, if an individual observes another to be energetic, and based on their past experience, they link an energetic person to intelligence, which they see as beneficial to their self-preservation, then the observer will likely infer that the other person is intelligent and therefore of value. Due to the complexity of human social behavior and the plethora of examples like the one above, each individual often approaches the social behavior process and need for acceptance in a unique way, which through our deeper understanding of the Hidden You is influenced by your family system, personality, and power persona. Therefore, we cannot conclude that one singular, implicit personality theory is utilized by all. However, there are some aspects of the social evaluation process that are consistent across all individuals or within group dynamics (Srivastava, Guglielmo, and Beer, 2010) (Kelley, 1988). One aspect of particular interest to our leadership psychology foundation is the need for acceptance within a group, and how the social evaluation process impacts group dynamics.

Before we continue, it should be abundantly clear by now that you must recognize your Hidden You and its impact on self-preservation and the need for acceptance. Understanding these concepts enables social and situational awareness, allowing you to facilitate an interaction where you can account for and neutralize your bias.

We previously reviewed the implicit personality theory and how it focuses on the patterns and bias formed by an individual. Now we must briefly explore how these patterns can impact group dynamics. One such proponent of this study was Harold

Kelley, an American social psychologist and professor of psychology at the University of California, Los Angeles. Kelley's work included the creation of the covariation model, an attribution theory in which people, or a group of people, make causal inferences to explain why other people behave a certain way (Kelley H. H., 1967) (Kelley H. H., *Attribution In Social Interaction,* 1971) (Kelley H. H., *Causal Schemata and the Attribution Process,* 1972) (Kelley H. H., *The Process of Causal Attribution,* 1973). Within group dynamics, the covariation model is concerned with both social perception and self-perception, where the degree in which you attribute social behaviors within the group is directed at the person as opposed to the situation (Kelley H. H., *Attribution Theory in Social Psychology*. In D. Levine (ed.), 1967) (Kelley H. H., *Attribution In Social Interaction,* 1971) (Kelley H. H., *Causal Schemata and the Attribution Process,* 1972) (Kelley H. H., *The Process of Causal Attribution,* 1973). In other words, within group dynamics, an individual's social perception and self-perception is often measured by group consensus, even when group consensus is based on speculation rather than reality. Understanding the covariation model, its effect on group dynamics, and its relationship with our self-preservation is a major reason why anyone who aspires to be a transcendent leader must have the basic tenets of leadership psychology built into their individual leadership foundation.

Socially, individuals have a fundamental need for positive and lasting relationships. People instinctively gravitate toward strength in numbers and take comfort in the company of others. It is our inborn self-preservation that drives our behavior to seek acceptance from like-minded individuals while drowning out or preventing outcomes that lead to fear and anxiety. In other words, when part of a group, we are more likely to accept the consensus view without ever inspecting for ourselves the validity or truth of what is being conveyed about a situation or an individual. As an alternative, a nonconsensus view may lead to rejection from the group.

Demonstrating this need, C. Nathan DeWall and coauthor Brad J. Bushman of Ohio State University provide an overview of social psychological research on the topic of social acceptance and rejection, where they describe the need to belong and how this need enabled early humans to fulfill their survival and reproductive goals. Per DeWall, "Although psychologists have been interested in close relationships and what happens when those relationships go awry for a very long time, it's only been about fifteen years that psychologists have been doing this work on exclusion and rejection" (DeWall, 2011). The results have highlighted just how central this form of social acceptance is to our lives and our subconscious self-preservation.

In the journal, DeWall describes how this inherent need to belong and be accepted is likely attributable to our primitive survival instincts handed down from our ancestors. DeWall reflects on how living in a group, and being accepted by the group, helped our ancestors survive harsh environments and provided safety and protection.

In direct contrast to acceptance, DeWall's research also addresses rejection and the importance of coping with rejection. DeWall states, "We should assume that everyone is going to experience rejection on a semi-regular basis throughout their life." He also states, "It's impossible to go through your entire life with everyone being respective and courteous to you all the time." When you are rejected or excluded, he says, "The best way to deal with it is to seek out other sources of friendship or other forms of acceptance" (DeWall, 2011).

DeWall describes how it is not uncommon for individuals who feel rejection to feel embarrassed and downplay the situation. However, when part of a group that has been rejected, our self-preservation and the need to resolve anxiety and fear becomes a collective mission. Contrary to individual rejection, to cope with group rejection, humans instinctively seek out others with similar fears and anxieties. DeWall states, "When people feel lonely, or when people feel excluded or rejected, these are things they can talk about." It is through this process of conformity and obedience, and the underlying need for acceptance or self-preservation, that we need to explore group dynamics and associated social behaviors.

As a transcendent leader, recognizing interdependencies between social behaviors and group dynamics is essential to lead an individual or a group. It is through this understanding, and the ability to care for others' self-preservation, that a leader develops a following that looks to them for guidance. Within this social evaluation process between leader and follower, each enters into a relationship of acceptance, a form of congenial self-preservation. Through various forms of successful interaction, the follower bestows a level of trust and acceptance that is influenced and psychologically cared for by the leader. The leader likewise forms a similar bond.

Once this level of trust and acceptance is achieved, a leader has the opportunity to gain future followers via the open and outward relationship represented by both the leader and the follower. It is this interaction that leads to the formation of a group, and it is the actions of both the leader and the followers that ultimately determine the group's success. From the interactions between the leader and the followers, a group dynamic or group culture forms. Within this group culture exists common social behaviors that represent the different types of followers and their respective Hidden Yous. Thus, understanding how different types of followers can influence the overall group dynamic is essential to your leadership foundation.

Robert E. Kelley developed a theory of how followers can influence a group and how they play an active role in group successes and failures. In his article "In Praise of Followers," Robert describes what he calls effective followers and nonfollowers (Kelley R. E., 1988). Effective followers are individuals who are considered to be enthusiastic, intelligent, ambitious, and self-reliant. Within effective followers there exist four main qualities. The first quality of an effective follower is the ability to self-manage—the ability to think critically, control your actions, and work independently. Robert's theory suggests it is important that followers manage themselves well, allowing the leader to delegate tasks to these individuals with confidence and no hesitation.

The second quality of an effective follower is commitment. To have commitment, an effective follower must be dedicated to the group's goal, vision, or cause. This is an important quality, as it facilitates raising individual morale and energy, which in turn raises the group's morale and energy.

The third quality of an effective follower is competence. Being competent facilitates the effective follower's ability to complete the goal or task for the group. It is not uncommon for competent effective followers to have above-average experience and skills.

The last of the four qualities is courage, the ability to hold true to your beliefs and uphold ethical standards, even when faced with dishonest or corrupt superior leaders.

To truly understand and appreciate group dynamics and be a transcendent leader, you must first learn how to be an effective follower. Built on the same concept of leadership transcendence, a transcendent follower also exudes a form of social behavior that is focused and committed to the self-preservation of their leader and the overall group. How a follower traverses the social evaluation process is dependent upon how they are perceived amongst the group dynamic that is formed.

Using Robert Kelley's follower theory, we can further differentiate the social behaviors associated with that of a follower versus a nonfollower. In his theory, he addresses two underlying dimensions that identify a key difference between the two. The first is whether the individual is an independent, critical thinker. The second is whether the individual is active or passive.

From these dimensions, Kelley has identified five types of followers (Kelley R. E., 1988). The first pattern is what Robert calls the "sheep." A sheep follower is an individual who is passive and requires external motivation. They often lack commitment and require constant supervision.

The second follower pattern is what Robert calls "yes-people." Yes-people are committed to the leader and the overall goal of the group. As yes-people followers, these individuals act as conformists and do not question the leader's decisions or actions. Yes-people followers will adamantly defend their leader when faced with opposition.

The third follower pattern is the "pragmatic." Followers that are pragmatic are not trailblazers or risk takers. Pragmatic followers often will not support controversial or unique ideas until a consensus has been recognized. It is not uncommon for a pragmatic follower to remain in the background.

Kelly describes the fourth pattern as the "alienated." These individuals are negative and often attempt to stall or bring the group down by questioning the leader's decisions. These individuals often view themselves as the rightful leader and are critical of the leader and fellow group members.

The last of the five follower patterns is the "star" follower. The star follower is an exemplary individual who is positive, active, and independent. Star followers will not blindly accept the decisions or actions of a leader until they have evaluated them. Furthermore, these types of followers can succeed without the presence of a leader.

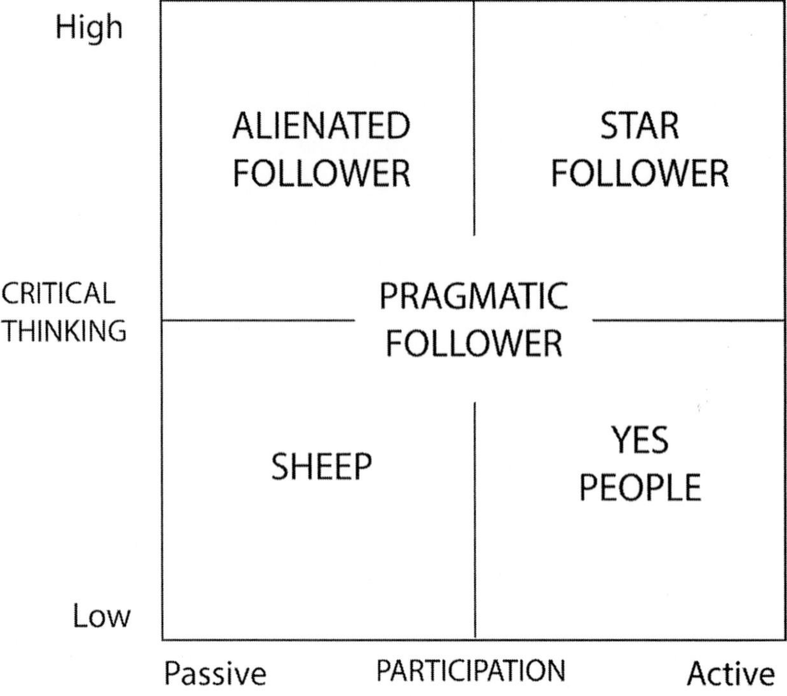

To solidify our understanding of how individual survival instincts and self-preservation influence social behavior as a transcendent follower and transcendent leader, Henry Alexander Murray and David Clarence McClelland provide additional insight into the correlation between our need for self-preservation and the impact this need has on the social behaviors that impact your ability to lead transcendently. David Clarence McClelland was an American psychologist noted for his work on motivation need theory (self-preservation), a theory that has recently been correlated to our inborn survival instinct and innate self-preservation. In McClelland's book *Human Motivation,* he described motivation as "a recurrent concern for a goal state or condition as measured in fantasy, which drives, directs, and selects the behavior of the individual" (McClelland, 1987). In this context, McClelland's term "fantasy" is what the Hidden You would describe as your perception of reality in relation to your survival instincts and self-preservation. McClelland's work was based on the work of Henry Alexander Murray, where McClelland expanded upon Murray's need theory through additional research and study.

To understand McClelland's need theory, we must first understand Murray's personology theory. Murray had a unique perspective, and as a result developed a theory called personology based on "need" and "press" (Murray, 1938). Murray defined a need as a force located somewhere in the brain that creates tension when aroused. We can now attribute this to our primitive survival instincts and our brain's three-tiered system. According to Murray, when a need is aroused, the person seeks goal objects that reduce the tension (e.g. fear and anxiety). Individuals learn to associate particular goal objects with the satisfaction of achieving certain needs (hardwired into our brain).

According to Murray, all people have the same basic psychological needs, but not to the same degree. Murray proposed that there is a hierarchy of needs, unique to each person, in which some of the needs are more important than others. When these instinctive needs are satisfied, the other needs then become more important. Unlike Maslow, Murray was focused only on psychological needs and their impact on human behavior.

Murray used a variety of methods to measure psychological needs, including self-report, questionnaires, interviews, observation of behavior, and projective techniques. The projective technique he, along with his colleague Christiana Morgan, developed is known as the thematic apperception test (TAT), which has been influential in research on personality and motivation. The TAT is a projective psychological test (Murray,

1938). Proponents of this technique assert that individual responses to the various narratives reveal their underlying motives, concerns, and perspectives. These in turn drive their social behavior. Historically, the TAT has been among the most widely researched, taught, and used of all projective psychological techniques. In *Explorations in Personality*, Murray states, "When a person interprets an ambiguous social situation he is apt to expose his own personality as much as the phenomenon to which he is attending . . . Each picture should suggest some critical situation and be effective in evoking a fantasy relating to it" (Murray, 1938).

Murray was focused on basic needs in personality, which he called psychogenic needs. He believed these needs were largely at the unconscious level (e.g. brain stem and limbic system). After significant research in this area, Murray narrowed these needs down, which vary depending on the time frame and the author. Below is the list of "psychogenic" needs identified in *Explorations in Personality*, edited by Henry A. Murray in 1938. This text, published by Oxford University Press in 1938, played a significant role in furthering the scientific study of human personality. Murray divided psychogenic needs into five groups.

Ambition Needs

Achievement	To overcome obstacles and succeed
Exhibition	To attract attention
Recognition	To gain approval and social status

Materialistic Needs

Acquisition	To obtain possessions
Retention	To keep things that have been acquired
Order	To make things clean, neat, and tidy
Construction	To build or create

Power Needs

Abasement	To surrender and accept punishment
Aggression	To forcefully overcome an opponent, controlling, taking revenge, or punishing them
Autonomy	To break free from constraints, resisting coercion and dominating authority; to be irresponsible and independent
Blame avoidance	To avoid blame and obey the rules
Contravariance	To oppose the attempted persuasion of others
Deference	To admire a superior person, praising them and yielding to them and following their rules
Dominance	To control your environment, controlling other people through command or subtle persuasion
Harm avoidance	To escape or avoid pain, injury, and death
Infavoidance	To avoid being humiliated or embarrassed to conceal a weakness

Status-Defense Needs

Counteraction	To make up for failure by trying again, prideful in seeking to overcome obstacles
Defendance	To defend yourself against attack or blame, hiding any failure of the self
Infavoidance	To avoid being humiliated or embarrassed

Affection Needs

Affiliation	To be close and loyal to another person, pleasing them and winning their friendship and attention
Nurturance	To help the helpless, feeding them and keeping them from danger
Play	To have fun, laugh, and relax, enjoying yourself
Rejection	To separate yourself from a negatively viewed object or person, excluding or abandoning it
Sex	To form relationship that leads to sexual intercourse
Succorance	To have your needs satisfied by someone or something; includes being loved, nursed, helped, forgiven, and consoled

Information Needs

Cognizance	To seek knowledge and ask questions about things in order to understand
Exposition	To provide information; educate others

Murray also contended that environmental forces play a significant role in your psychogenic needs. He called the environmental forces "press," referring to the pressure that will force you to act. Murray further theorized a difference between the real environmental forces, which he referred to as the "alpha press," and those that are merely perceived, the "beta press." This can also be described as or attributed to the conscious and subconscious mind.

Murray's need theory's ideas and methods of research are important because of their influence on subsequent theorists and researchers. His work laid the foundation for more in-depth studies in areas such as leadership. This is especially relevant to the continued research and studies associated with leadership, and how the need for power, affiliation, and achievement impacts overall leadership psychology. A significant contribution to these continued studies was carried out by the pioneering research work of the Harvard Psychological Clinic in the 1930s, summarized in Murray's *Explorations in Personality*. It provided the starting point for future studies of personality, especially those relating to needs and motives, which have been beneficial to the advancement of leadership psychology.

David C. McClelland's progress in association with Murray's original work as it relates to achievement motivation greatly influenced the continued progression of leadership psychology. McClelland was interested in understanding how individuals can be deliberately motivated so he could explain how individuals express their preferences for particular outcomes. In this connection, McClelland's theory is based on the idea that the need for achievement refers to an individual's preference for success in a competitive context. The vehicle McClelland employed to establish the presence of an achievement motive was the type of fantasy a person expressed on the thematic apperception test (TAT).

In 1961 McClelland published *The Achieving Society,* which articulated his model of human motivation. In his publication,

McClelland expands upon and ultimately popularizes Murray's psychogenic needs by developing the three needs theory. According to McClelland, these motivators are learned and influenced by our life experiences. McClelland's need theory (learned need theory) focused on these three particular motives: the need for achievement (nAch), the need for affiliation (nAff), and the need for power (nPow) (McClelland D. C., 1961).

The need for achievement is the desire to excel via a set of standards or guidelines. Those with a significant need for achievement often demonstrate a consistent concern for meeting obligations and accomplishing tasks. They tend to be more focused on internal motivation than external rewards. For example, those motivated by a high need for achievement are more likely to value intelligence and personal achievement over recognition and praise. Their need for achievement is what drives them to succeed.

The need for affiliation is the innate desire to build and experience strong and close personal relationships. Those with a high need for affiliation often have a larger social circle or are members of social groups. They tend to spend a significant amount of time interacting through conversation in person, over the phone, or via social media. Those with a need for affiliation are more likely to be members of social groups or clubs. They are also more likely to experience a strong form of loneliness or rejection compared to those with a low need for affiliation. Their need may be related to their sense of self and their innate desire for external stimulation and acceptance.

The need for power is the desire to be influential and to be perceived as having an impact on a group or organization. The need for power is associated with the desire or need to impact others, control the outcome, or be in a position of influence. Research has found that those with a high need for power have an innate desire for conformity and obedience. Similar to the Commander power persona, those with a need for power have shown a tendency to favor those who agree with them or favor their ideals.

McClelland's three needs are nonsequential and are used in relation to each other. McClelland theorized that these three needs are at the center of human motivation. His theory suggests that individuals do not have just one need, but a mixture of needs. Individuals with a significant need for achievement have an attraction to situations that entail and offer personal accountability. Individuals with a dominating need for authority and power often have a desire to influence and to increase personal status and prestige. Individuals that possess a great need for affiliation value building strong relationships and belonging to groups or organizations.

Through his research, McClelland concluded that each need and the relative importance of each will vary among individuals and groups. McClelland theorized and believed that if you know how an outstanding performer thinks and acts, you could replicate their performance by helping them learn how to properly think and act. In McClelland's journal publication "Managing Motivation to Expand Human Freedom," he believed that "understanding human motivation ought to be a good thing. It should help us to find out what we really want so that we can avoid chasing rainbows that are not for us. It should open up opportunities for self-development if we apply motivational principles to pursuing our goals in life" (McClelland D. C., 1978).

In addition to understanding your Hidden You, it is equally important to understand that of others. Today's society provides many opportunities to observe and evaluate the basic tenets of leadership psychology as described in this book. One of my favorite activities to further explore and observe these basic tenets is through the abundance of reality television shows.

Two of my favorite shows are *The Apprentice* and *Big Brother*. These are two diverse shows that expose everyday human interactions, exposing survival instincts and the need for self-preservation. Most remarkable is how these shows allow us to witness the social behaviors and social interactions through the prism of each individual and through the development of existing group dynamics. As I observe these shows, I identify the followers and the nonfollowers. Of these followers, who is an effective follower? Do any of the participants represent the sheep, yes-people, pragmatic, alienated, or are they the star follower?

Through a basic understanding of the tenets of leadership psychology, we now have a better understanding of how the Hidden You of an individual or a group influences overall success or failure. It is through the common studies of social, behavioral, and cognitive psychology as it relates to leadership psychology that we can better understand leadership through this unique prism. With a solid Hidden You analysis in place, to include a new understanding and appreciation for how individual needs impact self-preservation, group-preservation, and the ability to transcendently lead, we will now explore the systematic approach of "move," "adapt," and "left behind," thus putting you on a direct path toward leadership transcendence.

SYSTEMATIC APPROACH TO LEADERSHIP TRANSCENDENCE

Everyone has a plan until they get punched in the face.

—Mike Tyson

In life, as in leadership, regardless of how much you plan, you will experience success, and you will most certainly experience failure. When it comes to transcendent leadership, there is no greater test to your self-transcendence than failure. When it comes to failure, what sets transcendent leaders apart from other leaders is not just the ability to have a plan, but the system they have in place that allows them to master the skills necessary to account for the unexpected, while also seeking to care for the self-preservation of all.

Mike Tyson's quote "Everyone has a plan until they get punched in the face" does not just represent the world of boxing; it also represents the world of leadership, and how the lack of a systematic approach reduces a leader's ability to achieve their desired outcomes.

In Mike Tyson's fight against Michael Spinks, he won in ninety-one seconds via a ruled knockout. This was unheard of at the time, as Spinks was an undefeated professional boxer and was considered the lineal champion. At the time, Tyson was also undefeated and held the championship belts of all three of the major sanctioning organizations. Going into the fight, neither Tyson nor Spinks contemplated defeat. Neither one was prepared for the success or failure that would follow. Their plan was to win. Neither had a system in place that would facilitate their next steps following the outcome, regardless of the result.

For a leader to avoid getting punched in the face, they must have a systematic approach in place to help drive overall environmental alignment within society's social behaviors and to ensure their Hidden You analysis lines up with their goals. Without a proper leadership foundation and systematic approach, you might as well jump in the ring with someone who has the punching power of Mike Tyson.

Mike Tyson was right. Without a systematic approach to leadership transcendence, you too can experience the type of punch to the face that leads to a complete breakdown of your limbic system and your cerebral analysis—the type of failure that leaves you feeling completely left behind and wondering, *What the hell just happened?*

Regardless of the activity, following any experience of success or failure, you will undoubtedly negate the significance of your success while consuming yourself in the failure. This reaction is instinctive. Until I truly grasped the concept of the Hidden You, I was always fascinated by just how much time we commit to contemplating a failure, while only spending a fraction of the time trying to understand and replicate a success. An important aspect of the Hidden You is that without understanding yourself and your fear of rejection, your instinct is to avoid rejection, seek acceptance, and consume yourself in the avoidance of failure.

In reality, success will ultimately be achieved through the process of experiencing failure. Now, I am not saying this is always the case. It's just that the odds of finding success in anything without having first experienced some form of failure is highly improbable. What sets a transcendent leader apart from other leaders is how they handle failure. Transcendent leaders embrace failure. Instead of running away from failure, they run right toward it. Transcendent leaders are eager to squeeze out every ounce of experience that comes from failure. To understand the relationship between leadership transcendence and failure, you must first understand some basic tenets of leadership failure.

Napoleon Hill was an American author whose literature tremendously contributed to personal success concepts. Prior to his death in 1970, his best-known work, *Think and Grow Rich* (1937), was published during the Great Depression and sold over 20 million copies. In writing this book, Hill was inspired by Andrew Carnegie (d. 1919) who, as his apprentice, challenged Hill to seek out the formula for success (Hill N., 1937). In 1908, Carnegie was among the most powerful men in the world, and he helped Hill by granting him access to some of the most successful people of his era. In his 1928 multivolume work *The Law of Success*, Hill describes how he studied the likes of Andrew Carnegie, Henry Ford, J. P. Morgan, John D. Rockefeller, Alexander Graham Bell, and Thomas Edison (Hill N., 1928).

Through studying some of the most successful businessmen of his time, Hill concluded that there are two forms of leadership. The first form of leadership, and what Hill described as the most effective, is "leadership by consent of, and with the sympathy of, the followers." Hill's second form is "leadership by force, without the consent and sympathy of followers" (Hill N., 1937). This can also be described as those who do not adhere to the "No Asshole Rule." Hill felt strongly that "leadership by consent of the followers is the only brand that can endure" (Hill N. , 1937).

In Hill's book, he identifies ten major causes of failure in leadership:

1. "Inability to organize details." In order to avoid the traps of failure, leaders need to have followers—star followers to whom they can delegate important tasks to achieve their outcomes.
2. "Unwillingness to render humble service." Before a leader can become a leader, they must first learn how to follow.
3. "Expectation of pay for what they know instead of what they do with that which they know." Just because you get the opportunity to fulfill a leadership role does not mean you are a leader.
4. "Fear of competition from followers." A transcendent leader must be able to recognize and overcome their own inborn instincts for self-preservation. What sets transcendent leaders apart from their peers is their innate desire to help others achieve success.

5. "Lack of imagination." A leader, through Hidden You analysis, is able to unlock not only their own ability to create, but that of their followers. Through effective cerebral analysis, you can suppress the inborn fears and anxieties of an individual or group, allowing for a greater focus on the task at hand to ensue.
6. "Selfishness." According to Hill, "The leader who claims all the honour for the work of his followers is sure to be met by resentment. The really great leader . . . is contented to see the honours, when there are any, go to his followers, because he knows that most men will work harder for commendation and recognition than they will for money alone."
7. "Intemperance." By intemperance, Hill refers to overindulgence in any pleasures, to include food, drink, drugs, gambling, or sex. A leader who cannot show self-constraint is no leader at all.
8. "Disloyalty." In leadership, disloyalty is a form of self-preservation. A leader who only looks out for their own self-preservation will not lead for long.
9. "Authority of leadership." The type of leader who leads through respect, rather than through fear and intimidation.
10. "Emphasis on title." To be a transcendent leader, you must recognize that no one is beneath you. Titles do not make the person; actions do.

What Hill discovered, and what our own experiences have confirmed, is that failure is a part of life. What sets leaders apart is how you deal with the adversity of failure. Without a systematic approach to effectively manage the many challenges associated with failure, both consciously and subconsciously, your ability to lead transcendently is exponentially harder to achieve. To help illustrate the type of outcome a leader can expect to achieve without a systematic approach to transcendent leadership, I will use an old wives' tale about a bull and a turkey.

A turkey is hoping to chat with a bull. The turkey and bull were close friends and had known each other for several years. At least once a week, the two of them got together at an oak tree in the middle of a big open pasture. Running right next to this great big oak tree was an old wooden fence. As the bull approached the turkey, he noticed that his buddy was sitting on the ground next to the fence. This was unusual, as the bull knew the turkey was in greater danger from predators when on the ground than in the air. Moreover, his buddy looked like he was knocking on death's door.

The bull said to the turkey, "What is wrong with you? You look awful!"

The turkey said, "I feel awful. I have not had anything to eat in over a week, and if I can't get to the top of that tree to find food, I am afraid I am going to die!"

"We can't let that happen! You are my best friend and I can't lose you!"

"I need to fly up to the top of this oak tree, but I don't have enough strength and energy to get there. I can't even get on top of this fence."

"I have an idea, but you are not going to like it very much!" said the bull. "Why don't you try eating a little of my bull dung? I have been told that it is extremely nutritious."

"No way!" the turkey said.

"What do you have to lose? You are going to die and I can't let that happen. Not on my watch."

"All right then, but you better not tell anyone!" Then the turkey began to eat a little bit of the bull dung. He could immediately feel the nutrients exploding through his body.

The turkey said with excitement, "It's working! I can feel it!" The bull pranced around, telling his buddy to eat more. The turkey proceeded to eat all the bull dung he could find.

With all the energy required now available, the turkey took flight. He ascended to the first branch, then the second, then the third, making his way to the very top. Then the turkey yelled down to the bull, "I made it! I can see food!"

Just then there was a loud *BOOM!* that echoed across the pasture—a gunshot! The turkey came crashing down the tree, branch by branch, and landed right in front of the bull, dead! Unfortunately for the turkey, out on the outskirts of the field was a turkey hunter. The hunter had shot the turkey right out of the tree. The bull was devastated!

What is the moral of this tale? Bullshit might get you to the top, but it will not keep you there!

To avoid being the turkey, it requires more than a plan; it requires a systematic approach to leadership transcendence. The remaining chapters are intended to provide a road map to achieving leadership transcendence in work and in life. Like any road map, there are many ways to reach your destination. Sometimes you can take a shorter path, and sometimes you must take the long way around. Regardless, it is through a systematic approach that you will find the most optimal path.

There will always be a road ahead or a tree to ascend. Given all the complexities associated with leadership and the interwoven social behaviors that accompany it, one lifetime is truly not enough for any individual to fully understand everything there is to know about leadership. One approach might work today, and not work tomorrow. That is what makes leading such an exciting adventure. It is through the systematic approach to leadership transcendence that you can stay the course, or when knocked off course, have a way of getting back on course and moving in the appropriate direction.

It is the lack of a Hidden You analysis that complicates how we communicate and interact. Whether it's through self-preservation, inborn survival instincts, or hierarchy, there will always be an imbalance in the world. I assure you, in your lifetime, this dynamic will never change! We are, after all, only human. Whether as a leader or a follower, we are all desperate for guidance, acceptance, and self-preservation. A basic fundamental principal associated with biology is that all species, when faced with a change in environment, have essentially three choices: move, adapt, or die. As part of the systematic approach to leadership transcendence, we will leverage this important framework in the form of "move," "adapt," or "left behind." For our purposes, "die" would insinuate that an opportunity to evolve as a transcendent leader is no longer available. To acknowledge this important difference between biology and our systematic approach, we will instead use the alternative "left behind." Being left behind insinuates that you can catch up, get better, and overcome existing challenges and adversity.

Regardless of where you are in your leadership evolution, your leadership evolution either just began or continued its journey the minute you started reading this book. Through the systematic approach of "move," "adapt," or "left behind," I will introduce a foundation for assessing and caring for the many common attributes associated with transcendent leadership. Always remember, true success is always a failure or two away! Therefore, you must embrace failure, cherish success, and leverage your new knowledge to help ensure the self-preservation for all.

MOVE

There is no such thing as perpetual tranquility of mind while we live here; because life itself is but motion, and can never be without desire, nor without fear, no more than without sense.

—Thomas Hobbes

As humans, we have been given a tremendous opportunity to spend what amounts to an extremely short period of time here on earth to include all the complexities the world around us has to offer. Through these complexities exist our inborn survival instincts to ensure our self-preservation. Also inherent to our self-preservation is the instinct to "move," the need for perpetual preparation through perpetual learning. Without movement, we conserve too much energy, and we become stagnant and susceptible to various things that seek to harm us. To create some balance as it relates to this instinct, and to experience life to its fullest, we must never cease to "move."

We are a species comprised of both matter and energy—energy derived from both chemical and electrical reactions. Regardless of your view of evolution or intelligent design, the energy and the power that went into your creation, from embryo to adulthood, until death and beyond, never truly ceases to exist. When our time is up, we can only take with us what we have learned and experienced.

For humans, the process of generating energy is complex and yet required for self-preservation. Our body's organs consume a lot of energy, and the most important organ in relation to leadership transcendence is our brain, which makes up 2 percent of a person's weight (Drubach, *The Brain Explained,* 2000). Despite its size in comparison to the whole body, even at rest, the brain consumes energy at ten times the rate of the rest of the body per gram of tissue. The average power consumption of a typical adult is one hundred watts, and the brain consumes 20 percent of this energy (*Macmillan Encyclopedia of Physics,* 1996). Therefore, the human brain consumes twenty watts of power.

There are numerous ways in which we create this energy. Mostly, we get it through food, which gives us chemical energy. This chemical energy is then transformed into kinetic energy, which is leveraged to power our muscles, organs, and most importantly, our brain. This is the energy required to effectively prepare through perpetual learning, and thus "move."

Albert Szent-Györgyi, a Hungarian biochemist, stated that "a living cell requires energy not only for all its functions, but also for the maintenance of its structure. Without energy, life would be extinguished instantaneously, and the cellular fabric would collapse" (Nobel Foundation, 1999, p. 440). This topic may seem odd and unexpected, but in order to achieve transcendent leadership, your health is an essential component. Exercise and healthy eating facilitate the body's ability to create energy, which is necessary to power all of the brain's important functions.

Step one to becoming a transcendent leader requires setting up an appropriate physical-exercise schedule. First, get a physical exam through a medical expert to ensure healthy participation. Second, set up an exercise routine through a local gym or through a private trainer. Through exercise and healthy eating, your health and energy will be proactively stimulated to drive the functions necessary for perpetual preparation and learning.

Your brain is no different than the rest of the muscles in your body. If you do not use your muscles, they become stagnant and less proficient. Similar to utilizing exercise to stimulate the growth of muscles, recent research has demonstrated that exercise increases growth factors in the brain, making it easier for the brain to grow new neuronal connections. You can actually achieve additional brain performance through physical exercise. The overall benefits of physical exercise, especially aerobic exercise, have a tremendous positive effect on brain function on multiple fronts, ranging from the molecular to the behavioral level.

Studies have shown that exercise facilitates information processing and memory, two functions essential to leading with transcendence. In 2003, two scientists by the name of Colcombe and Kramer analyzed the results of eighteen scientific studies published between 2000 and 2001 that were conducted with both an exerciser group and a nonexerciser group, each having similar exercise profiles. The results of this meta-analysis showed that fitness training increased the cognitive performance in healthy adults between the ages of fifty-five and eighty (Colcombe and Kramer, 2003). Another meta-analysis published in 2004 by Heyn and colleagues showed similar beneficial effects on people who were over sixty-five years old and who had cognitive impairment or dementia (Heyn, Abreu, and Ottenbacher, 2004).

To capture additional evidence associated with the effect of exercise on the human brain, another study done by the scientist S. J. Colcombe leveraged MRI technology to look at the effect of fitness on the human brain. In 2006, Colcombe randomly assigned fifty-nine older adults to either a cardiovascular aerobic exercise group or to a nonaerobic exercise control group (stretching and toning exercise) (Colcombe, et al., 2006). Participants were put through an exercise program where they would exercise three hours per week for six months. Colcombe and his team scanned the participants' brains before and after the training period. Following six months of coordinated exercise, when compared to the nonaerobic group, the brain volume of the aerobic-exercising group increased in several areas. Overall increases in volume occurred within the frontal and temporal areas of the brain, the areas involved in cerebral analysis and memory processes. The researchers were not able to conclude what underlying cellular changes might have caused these changes. However, through various past animal-research studies, they concluded that the changes may be due to an increased number of blood vessels and an increased number of connections between neurons.

As we explored through Hidden You analysis and the chemical reactions associated with pleasure and fear, exercise initiates the release of additional hormones, all of which contribute to a healthy environment which helps to stimulate the growth of new brain cells. From a social-behavioral perspective, exercise helps to reduce the chemical reaction that naturally occurs when experiencing fear and anxiety.

As humans, we are surrounded by energy. As part of the systematic approach to leadership transcendence, using this energy to "move" is essential and never wanes. Whether it's becoming a transcendent leader or mastering a difficult situation, recognizing and applying the tenets of "move" is essential to your leadership evolution.

CHAPTER 6

PERPETUAL PREPARATION

By failing to prepare you are preparing to fail.
—Benjamin Franklin

For most species, if not all, migrations begin with preparation. How are migrations relevant to leadership transcendence and your leadership evolution?

A leadership evolution does not happen overnight. Like most things in life, it takes time and requires continuous preparation. To ensure a successful migration, perpetual preparation is the key to a successful "move."

As the first component of our systematic approach, "move" represents the need for perpetual preparation or perpetual learning. How you choose to learn is not as important. Stagnation, or a "woe is me" attitude, is not an acceptable approach within this strategy. What's important is that learning and consuming new information regarding leadership is continuous.

During the last fifty years, advances in science and technology have had a tremendous impact on learning needs and styles, where our ability to quickly identify and consume information has advanced exponentially. No longer do we just acquire knowledge through schools and institutions. Today, learning can take place anywhere and at any time. Through technology, such as smartphones and tablets, we have tools that facilitate our daily interactions with others and with the world around us. Never before has self-directed learning been so abundant.

As part of "move," not only is self-directed learning required, you must establish study circles to share new experiences with others. Through study circles, you can interact with leaders who share in the same desire of achieving transcendence. Study circles are essential to receiving 360-degree and situational feedback that represents what you need to hear, not what you want to hear. This feedback will reflect your true strengths and weaknesses, thus facilitating your ability to continue to learn and grow.

Oscar Ulrik Bernhardin Olsson, of Sweden, is regarded as the father of study circles (Larson and Nordvall, 2010). He created the first study circle in 1902 as part of the International Order of Good Templars. Its purpose was to organize in small groups to discuss topics where study material was rare, and where discussion of such topics did not occur in everyday conversation. They provided the opportunity for healthy debate, and through proper consideration for others, the ability to accept feedback with humility, all of which are attributes that are essential to leadership transcendence.

In becoming a transcendent leader, it is essential to have a study circle, a place where information, feedback, and lessons learned can be shared in confidence and with the intent of achieving greater insight regarding your strengths and weaknesses. A place where 360-degree feedback can be shared freely, where one's inborn concern for self-preservation can be checked at the door. In becoming a transcendent leader, information and feedback is vital to the overall systematic approach and your ability to identify your weaknesses. These areas require a greater focus for learning and perpetual preparation. Without perpetual preparation, stagnation sets in, and it becomes much harder to react to situations requiring transcendent leadership.

Through the game of golf, we can explore the odds of hitting a hole-in-one to demonstrate how through perpetual preparation, you can generate better odds of achieving transcendent leadership.

The odds of a professional golfer hitting a hole-in-one is 2,500 to 1 (Kerr-Dineen, 2010). For comparison, the odds of highly experienced, transcendent leaders successfully aligning themselves with the combination of their inborn survival instincts and need for self-preservation, while also applying interactions that align to a recipient's personality, while communicating in such a way that the recipient can successfully use cerebral analysis to process the information needed to achieve a desired outcome, will invariably be less than favorable. If the last sentence is overwhelming, then it does a good job of depicting just how complex the human social-evaluation process can be. In more simple terms, regardless of your experience and leadership skill, the odds of hitting this metaphorical hole-in-one are exponentially greater than those of a professional golfer hitting an actual hole-in-one. To be clear, this is not to infer that you have no chance; it just means that if we confront reality, we can truly begin to see the magnitude of the complexity inherent within our social behaviors and our inability to effectively and reliably communicate. Through perpetual preparation, and by applying a systematic approach to building our leadership foundation, we can increase our odds of creating an environment where intended outcomes have the greatest chance of being realized.

By not understanding the importance of "move" as part of a systematic approach, where no perpetual preparation or leadership foundation is available, transcendent leadership will be difficult to achieve. Without a systematic approach that encourages you to "move," the odds of hitting a leadership transcendence hole-in-one become increasingly unfavorable, while the odds of becoming the "turkey" from the story become more favorable. For simple comparison, an amateur golfer's odds of hitting a hole-in-one is 12,500 to 1—five times less likely to occur than that of a professional golfer (Kerr-Dineen, 2010). If we label a leader with no leadership foundation as an amateur (or turkey), and we apply this same lack of leadership foundation to a group of amateur leaders, the odds of such leaders not achieving any desired outcome go up exponentially.

To substantiate the importance of what it means to "move," an important first question for anyone who seeks to be a transcendent leader is "Why should anyone be led by me?" It is not uncommon for any leader when asked this question to stumble and struggle with giving an answer. Why wouldn't they? Our inborn self-preservation is not structured to think in these terms. Self-preservation is about the individual, not the group. Additionally, we are not taught to recognize that leadership is a skill, and that to master any skill, you must be willing to "move."

In a *Harvard Business Review* article written by Robert Goffee and Gareth Jones titled "Why Should Anyone Be Led By You?" they addressed this question by identifying four unique qualities of what they called inspirational leaders, a form of leadership transcendence (Goffee and Jones, 2000):

1. "They selectively show their weakness." Inspirational leaders are not afraid to show their vulnerabilities, which makes them more authentic.
2. "They rely heavily on intuition to gauge appropriate timing and course of their action." Inspirational leaders don't fear failure and are comfortable in trusting their instincts.
3. "They manage employees with something we call tough empathy." Inspirational leaders are not afraid to be transparent and direct in their feedback with their followers, while at the same time rolling up their sleeves to help their followers succeed.
4. "They reveal their differences." Inspirational leaders are able to embrace what differentiates them from the pack, and they openly accept their difference as a strength.

For each quality, think about the context for which the authors are conveying their message. Think about all the subtle attributes and complexities, the overall knowledge, and the lessons learned, and through this applied experience facilitate the need to "move." This type of "move," which over time and through successful "mastery" or self-actualization invokes the need for "self-transcendence," ultimately inspires the need to pass this information on to others. This facilitates the type of leadership evolution that can only be accomplished through understanding the need to "move."

According to Robert Goffee and Gareth Jones, there are four popular myths about leadership. The first myth is that "Everyone can be a leader" (Goffee and Jones, 2000). In their observations, they determined not everyone can be a leader. Not everyone has the required knowledge or developed actualization. They concluded that individuals must want to be leaders and that many talented individuals are just not interested in the inherent level of responsibility. The authors also pointed out that some individuals would prefer to devote more time to their personal lives than to work.

Personally, and as previously stated, I believe everyone can become a transcendent leader or learn how to apply inspirational leadership attributes as previously described. Not all leaders are anointed or at the top of the hierarchy. Without perpetual preparation, without a study circle and desire to achieve new leadership knowledge, I do not disagree with Goffee and Jones's observations. To become a transcendent leader, an individual must recognize the need for self-actualization via a continuous migration and the need for establishing their own leadership evolution. Without the knowledge and the inherent understanding of what it takes to become an inspirational leader, or how to effectively manage and connect with people, leadership transcendence is hard to achieve.

Goffee and Jones also addressed the myth that "People who get to the top are leaders" (Goffee and Jones, 2000). In this portion of the study, they determined that not all people who get to the top are leaders and not all leaders are at the top. Throughout any organization, you will find individuals who, through their own natural leadership ability or through their own inborn desire to "move," have become effective leaders.

Unfortunately, in today's working environment, more often than not, people at the top are not transcendent leaders, and more closely resemble "turkeys." This can be attributed to the fact that most individuals in these roles have not begun their Hidden You analysis as part of their leadership evolution, and there is no mentor encouraging them to "move." In these circumstances, it is not uncommon for many of these individuals to reach the top via their inborn political acumen. In many ways this ability to adapt is to be commended. Whether these individuals recognize it or not, more often than not, they are applying a form of adaptation, albeit often in the form of bull dung. They have mastered the ability to "adapt" by applying a form of influence on others that most often produces an outcome for their own self-preservation.

While it may feel counterintuitive, this inherent attribute is in many ways to be admired. With the recognition and inclusion of Hidden You analysis and a systematic approach, these inherent capabilities can be harnessed and leveraged to exponentially enhance your reputation as a true transcendent leader. For those who lack these inherent capabilities or personality traits, recognizing the importance of situational awareness and the art of influence is an extremely important step in your leadership evolution.

Goffee and Jones determined that not all "leaders deliver business results" (Goffee and Jones, 2000). They state, "If results were always a matter of good leadership, picking leaders would be easy." This observation speaks directly to the need for a systematic approach to leadership transcendence. Regardless of success or failure, the outcome is not always a reflection of your leadership skills as a whole. Some things are just unpredictable, and how unexpected events impact the overall outcome is not always within a leader's control.

The fourth myth addressed by Goffee and Jones is that all leaders "are great coaches" (Goffee and Jones, 2000). In their research and observations, they concluded that it is rare to find leaders who are good at coaching others. That's not to say that great leaders cannot be great coaches. Leadership, management, and coaching are all skills that must be learned. However, like many attributes associated with humans, some people are naturally more gifted than others. This is certainly true when it comes to coaching, teaching, or connecting with others. Counterintuitively, not all individuals have an innate desire to lead or coach.

In my experience, the desire to lead is a byproduct of your Hidden You. Transcendent leaders recognize this desire and the inherent internal struggle of not knowing what it truly means to lead. Truly great leaders inherently recognize the complex world of leadership. They recognize the critical importance of perpetual preparation, and they proactively seek to better understand the unique attributes and qualifications associated with true leadership. In other words, they are always on the "move."

CHAPTER 7

IT'S A PROCESS, NOT AN EVENT

Before one can hit a grand-slam home run, it first requires singles, doubles, or triples.

—Unknown

Like most things in life, it takes time to learn the many different methodologies, techniques, and best practices for becoming an effective and transcendent leader. A whole industry has been built on this subject. So much information is available that you could spend a lifetime trying to consume it all. To continue your leadership evolution, you must at least make a concerted effort to consume it. While this is not an achievable task, it is the concept, the recognition, and constant pursuit of consuming this knowledge, which will play a critical role in your ability to successfully lead.

One of the more important capabilities we have is the ability to use cerebral analysis to reason and make good decisions regarding our self-preservation. This ability is fostered by our ability to learn. Through an inherent learning process, in combination with real events, we are genetically programmed to use this continuous learning to make decisions to facilitate our own survival. George Leonard, author of the book *Mastery: The Keys To Success and Long-Term Fulfillment,* captured the essence of how this ability is maximized over time through experience and what he ultimately describes as mastery. George Leonard describes mastery as follows:

"It resists definition yet can be instantly recognized. It comes in many varieties, yet follows certain unchanging laws. It brings rich rewards, yet is not really a goal or a destination but rather a process, a journey. We call this journey mastery, and tend to assume that it requires a special ticket available only to those born with exceptional abilities. But mastery isn't reserved for the super talented or even for those who are fortunate enough to have gotten an early start. It's available to anyone who is willing to get on the path and stay on it—regardless of age, sex, or previous experience" (Leonard, 1992).

The challenge with mastering your leadership evolution is that there are few, if any, road maps or systematic approaches to guide us on this leadership journey or to illuminate the right path. As much as we appreciate the advancement of science and technology, these advancements can also be distractions toward achieving mastery. We're continually bombarded with "Generation Now" priorities, and "promises of immediate gratification, instant success, and fast, temporary relief, all of which lead in exactly the wrong direction" (Leonard, 1992).

Along these same lines, George Leonard goes on to describe an existing world where most are seeking the quick-fix, an anti-mastery mentality that disrupts our society and subsequent social behaviors. This, in many ways, is what is wrong with leadership today. It's "things" such as money and misguided ambition that drive individuals into leadership roles. However, the idea of needing to learn how to lead takes a backseat to financial results and self-gratification. The void of leadership and the lack of expectations of actually having to lead have created an environment where results outweigh the migration and mastery of the leadership evolution itself. This in turn creates a vicious cycle that not only prevents leaders from developing and reaching their potential, but also threatens their health, education, career, and relationships. This cycle hinders the self-prescribed leader, their company, and ultimately the success and self-preservation of the followers.

Unlike many other professions where students are purposefully subjected to environments and circumstances designed to facilitate an expedited mastery of their craft on a daily occurrence, leadership growth is most often subjected to a different time table. The ability to truly master leadership transcendence is debatable. Regardless, you must first be in a position or a role that facilitates your ability to experience the opportunity to lead others.

It is important to recognize that the process of consuming information, and then applying such knowledge to real-world events in the form of reason and sound decisions, is a process and not an event. It is important to recognize and accept that your leadership evolution takes time, and through perpetual preparation and the pursuit of knowledge, you will be better prepared to handle the many forms of leadership and management situations that require strong reasoning.

In the book *Outliers*, author Malcolm Gladwell says that it takes roughly ten thousand hours of practice to achieve mastery in a field (Gladwell, 2008). Through his research in the social sciences, where he focuses on areas such as sociology, psychology, and social psychology, Malcolm Gladwell's books and articles deal with the unexpected implications and outcomes associated with human social behaviors. If his conclusion is true, how can we leverage this knowledge to facilitate your leadership journey toward achieving leadership transcendence?

As you start your leadership evolution, and over time experience both trials and tribulations, it is the actual systematic approach and the mastery of the leadership evolution that will ultimately prevail and best position you to be the most likely to survive any challenging situation as a transcendent leader. Those who have inherently understood the importance and have begun their own "move" don't just work harder than everybody else. At some critical point in time, these intuitive, self-motivated leaders fell in love with the practice of learning to lead—to the point that they want to do little else.

A comparison would be a professional basketball player who, after team practice, stays in the gym and will not leave until he makes a thousand shots. A software developer who spends all day developing code, and after leaving work goes home to write more open-source software on their own time. The football player who spends all day on the practice field with teammates, and after practice goes to the film room or heads home to study game tapes. Those who excel and reach mastery status are in love with what they do, and at some point it no longer feels like work. More importantly, they achieved mastery, or a form of self-actualization through a systematic approach, and through the tenets of "move!"

ADAPT

The measure of intelligence is the ability to change.
— Albert Einstein

A major factor in achieving leadership transcendence or finding any comfort amongst the chaos associated with human social behaviors that permeate our society is within your ability to "adapt." Without the ability to "adapt," a leader is likely to succumb to life's many challenges that often manifest from our inborn instincts and the need for self-preservation that, when in conflict with our cerebral analysis, are converted to paralyzing internal fears. Central to combating these fears and to ensure you are always on the right path toward leadership transcendence is the systematic approach as it relates to the ability to "adapt."

When it comes to any form of leadership, every aspect of success or failure can be directly attributed to the ability or inability to "adapt." In fact, if we collected all literature ever written regarding leadership, we would conclude that at the highest level of interpretation, the key component to successful leadership is based on the ability to "adapt."

To help solidify our leadership foundation, the first half of this book was all about the Hidden You and how knowing your Hidden You allows you to better understand the complexities of human social behaviors. The Hidden You analysis represents how your personality and power personas are interpreted within the big fish bowl of complex personalities that coexist on earth. Without the ability to discover your Hidden You, it is difficult to assess, much less achieve, the ability to understand and apply the instrumental qualities of enhanced communications that best strengthen your Hidden You weaknesses. Without assessing or recognizing these weaknesses, the ability to successfully influence and "adapt" to the myriad of personalities and subsequent human conflicts born out of bad communication and the need for self-preservation becomes difficult to achieve.

As part of this systematic approach to leadership transcendence, the first phase addressed "move," the need for learning past, present, and future concepts associated with leadership, and the process for mastering all of the various concepts and techniques that facilitate a transcendent leader's ability to achieve desired outcomes and the self-preservation for all.

When it comes to the systematic approach to transcendent leadership, there are fundamental concepts and instrumental qualities of enhanced communication that, through perpetual preparation and in association with the need to "move," are essential to the ability to learn and grow.

To achieve mastery, we must explore how influence, in conjunction with the qualities of enhanced communication, facilitates the ability to "adapt" and drive the type of positive change and positive social interaction that leads to leadership transcendence.

Throughout this component of the systematic approach to leadership transcendence, we will explore the more relevant tenets of "influence" and the instrumental qualities of enhanced communication that facilitate the ability to be an effective and transcendent leader. We will explore how these qualities impact your perception as a leader, your ability to influence your own leadership, and your ability to influence those needing to be led. It is through the proper use of such qualities that a transcendent leader can achieve desired outcomes for the self-preservation of all.

CHAPTER 8

INFLUENCE—TOP DOWN, BOTTOM UP, AND INSIDE OUT

Your present circumstances don't determine where you can go; they merely determine where you start.

—Nido Qubein

There is no other subject within the "move," "adapt," or "left behind" system that is of greater significance than "influence." When things don't go our way, we assess our current situation as being in direct conflict with our expectations and desire for success. This is especially true when dealing with perceived failure or inherent weakness. Our instinct is to focus on the negative, without giving conscious thought to how our circumstance is impacting our ability to learn and grow. So often when mentoring leaders today, I have to remind them that the trials and tribulations they experience today make them more valuable going forward. As transcendent leaders, it is only through understanding the power of influence that our circumstances become manageable.

When it comes to leadership evolution, the mastery of learning how to influence, how to accept the process of being influenced, and how to accept the outcome of intended influential measures, favorable or unfavorable, will play a significant role in your ability to be an effective and transcendent leader. There is no finite moment in leadership. Leadership, especially transcendent leadership, represents an infinite cycle where you are continuously observing and applying various forms of influence in order to achieve intended outcomes. This understanding, in culmination with everything we have learned thus far, has facilitated our need to capture the importance of influence within the systematic approach of "adapt."

When a leader is responsible for making decisions for the collective whole, it is true that the amount of influence required to initiate such decisions can be minimal when compared to the decision-making process at the lower levels. However, regardless of where you reside—at the top, middle, or bottom of the hierarchy—your ability to influence positive change never ceases to exist. Whether you are having to influence top down, bottom up, or inside out, the same Hidden You analysis is required. It is through this understanding that we debunk the myth of having to be at the top of the hierarchy in order to create desired change.

On the surface, it is easy to understand how this perception is often created. Within the nucleus of this myth exists one constant, and that is the element of time. As we explored in Chapter 2, "Generation Now" has a profound impact on our expectations. It has created a lack of patience and an expectation that everything must be achieved as fast as humanly possible. This has also led to the perception that as a leader, the only way to achieve a desired outcome is to be the one making all the decisions.

When it comes to leadership transcendence and your ability to influence desired outcomes, the time it takes to achieve this outcome cannot be manipulated. Any attempt to manipulate time to achieve an outcome based on influence that resides outside its own natural occurrence will invariably be nontranscendent and will most often yield an undesirable outcome.

Through our inborn self-preservation, this is a difficult concept to understand and accept. It is our inborn instincts and the "Generation Now" that consciously and subconsciously tell us we have to have our desired outcome at the time most beneficial to our own internal needs. Complicating matters is our subconscious self-preservation and desire to be at the top, and we often invariably lose sight of the bigger picture and therefore lack patience and resolve. To be a transcendent leader, you must come to recognize the element of time and the ability, through applying instrumental qualities of enhanced communication, to allow the outcome of influence to materialize within its own universal timeframe. This essentially allows the outcome to come to fruition without being forced or manipulated through shortcuts. That is not to insinuate that you cannot eventually yield more efficient intended outcomes as a result of applying a more effective use of instrumental qualities of enhanced communication.

Several successful books, trade magazines, and articles have been dedicated to the ability to influence, many of which address common related attributes such as being trustworthy, honest, respectful, encouraging, a good role model, and having a positive attitude. In your leadership evolution and the systematic approach to leadership transcendence, we will only focus on three basic tenets that fall outside these common attributes.

The first basic tenet, which we have addressed, is the acceptance that the need to avoid manipulating time is counterintuitive to our inborn instincts, yet essential to leadership transcendence.

The second basic tenet is the inherent need to create and satisfy your perpetual curiosity. Curiosity is another form of "move," as it is through curiosity that we find the motivation to learn new things, and without "move," there is no curiosity. Of all the most influential people to have walked this earth or who continue to walk the earth today, the one trait they all possess is a keen sense of curiosity. To be an effective influencer, you must seek curiosity in all things.

Curiosity is not just associated with influencing others. Curiosity applies to all things. To be influential, to drive social behaviors that care for the subconscious inborn need to feel secure in your self-preservation, it's your curiosity that will facilitate a mutually beneficial interaction. You must explore all of the various subjects that are relevant to today's societal activities. No subject is off limits. It is curiosity and the need to consistently be on the "move" that is essential to your ability to "adapt" while leveraging the various forms of influence.

You must spend time each day or throughout each week fulfilling your curiosity on subjects outside the subject you are trying to influence. Whether it is through books, both written or audio, television documentaries, trade magazines, or the Internet, you must seek perpetual curiosity to achieve leadership transcendence.

The third basic tenet of influence is the need to be influenced. Just as you must first learn to follow before you can truly lead, the same applies to influence. Before you can master the skill of influence, you must first master the skill of knowing when you are being influenced and how to embrace it.

Being influenced often goes against our perceived culture and inborn instincts. In the world of leadership, there exists a perception that being influenced is bad, and that it is better to influence than to be influenced. As we explored leadership genes in Chapter 4, we discovered how our family system and upbringing plays an influential role in the development of our personality and perspective. Your Hidden You, just like society's collective Hidden You, is a result of the many influences and experiences that have been absorbed within the family system over many generations. As such, your current Hidden You perspectives, your thoughts, and your ideas on how to successfully navigate society are a result of those experiences.

Through self-preservation, just as we focus more on our failures than our successes, we have been hardwired to fear and avoid being influenced. A common example that has been engrained in our minds from an early age are the dangers in being influenced to use illegal drugs. Any such form of peer pressure is a great representation of what we would consider a bad influence. Over time, culture and society determined that being influenced is bad. On the contrary, there are actually many cases where being influenced is quite helpful. A basic understanding of what influence is and how to recognize it can help you leverage the many benefits that being influenced has to offer.

As part of "influence" and social perception, a term used to describe how influence affects perception is "perceptual set." Perceptual set refers to a predisposition to perceive things in a certain way based on past experiences or expectations. Similar to the covariation model discussed in Chapter 5, we tend to notice only certain aspects of a "thing" or situation, while ignoring other details. In other words, there are many distractions, social behaviors, and group dynamics that can interfere with our perceptual set. By being able to confront the reality of any given perceptual set within the social, political, spiritual, and economic systems of society, you will be better equipped to lead transcendently. Additionally, to confront the reality of your perpetual set, you must be influenceable.

To better understand the concept of being influenceable, we must revisit the concept of a star follower. Star followers will not blindly accept the decisions or actions of a leader until they have evaluated them completely. Additionally, these types of followers can succeed without a leader's guidance. Star followers, by nature, recognize the importance of being influenceable and how to leverage this subconscious attribute to help their leader achieve desired outcomes. They recognize that they must fulfill the role that best ensures the self-preservation of all.

Through social behaviors such as the perceptual set and the covariation model, a form of social networking will manifest within an organization or group. Influenceable followers are able to influence the perceptual set of individuals or groups, as well as use the covariation model to enable transcendent leaders to influence the mindshare of existing and new followers.

To further expand on the concept of being influenceable, social-network theorists Duncan J. Watts, a professor of sociology at Columbia University, and Peter Sheridan Dodds, an assistant professor of mathematics and statistics at the University of Vermont, conducted social-networking research and introduced their findings in the article "Influentials, Networks, and Public Opinion Formation" (Duncan and Dodds, 2007). The purpose of their research was to help capture logically and mathematically how influential people within social networks and group dynamics can disseminate and reach conformity of an "idea." Additionally, their goal was to capture a formula for helping to determine how many individuals it takes within social networks or group dynamics to reach overall alignment of this "idea."

Due to the complexities of trying to recreate real-world scenarios associated with social networking and group dynamics, Watts and Dodds had to develop several models where they varied the influenceable percentages from one individual to another, so some individuals were highly influenceable while others were less influenceable. Additionally, for each model, they would vary how many connections or relations an individual would have with other individuals within the social network or group dynamic. Through model-simulation results, Watts and Dodds would compare models to examine how deep and wide an idea would spread depending on whether it started with an individual who was influenceable or noninfluenceable.

As we have come to recognize through the complexity in the Hidden You, various types of research have proven it difficult to capture Hidden You complexities within a simulation of real-world scenarios. However, regardless of this challenge, there are some observations that can be leveraged to help researchers derive conclusions from these types of studies. In this case, Watts and Dodds captured a key attribute associated with being influenceable.

They concluded that the probability of a successful influence was more dependent upon the number of influenceables than it was on the influencers. They determined that the influencing of an "idea" would reach critical mass much quicker if an "idea" was positioned with influenceables first, thus fostering an environment where other influencables were more likely to reach conformity or, in some extreme cases, groupthink, described by Wikipedia as "a psychological phenomenon that occurs within a group of people in which the desire for harmony or conformity in the group results in an irrational or dysfunctional decision-making outcome" (Wikipedia, Groupthink, n.d.). Regardless of the actual result, irrational or rational, the greater number of influenceables would yield exponentially greater success for the conformity of an idea within the social network or group dynamics. Dodds stated that "in the end, you don't have control over how people spread your message." However, the best way to use influenceables to disseminate and reach conformity is to give the idea or desired outcome "social worth." In other words, an idea must confront reality and reflect the self-preservation for all.

To achieve support of leadership transcendence and develop a strong social network and healthy group dynamic that facilitates influenceable star followers, it is important to understand some common aspects of what is called "interpersonal influence." Interpersonal influence is a type of social influence that results from group members encouraging, or forcing, conformity while discouraging, and possibly punishing, nonconformity (Forsyth, 2010).

Stanley Schachter was an American social psychologist who documented the effects of interpersonal influence. In his research on rejection, deviance, and communication (1951), Schachter conducted an experiment where he identified three soldiers, where within a group of soldiers, each identified soldier would perform a role as defined by Schachter. As part of the experiment, the first soldier played the role of what Schacter called the "mode." The "mode" took the side of the participants from the beginning, consciously choosing an option consistently on the less-disruptive side of conformity, and whose role it was to consistently agree with the majority of ideas within the group dynamics (Wesselman, 2014). The second soldier played the role of the "deviant," which was the most extreme position within the experiment. It was the "deviant's" role to always disagree. The third soldier played the role of what Schachter called the "slider." The "slider's" role was to gradually be persuaded so that at the end of the discussion he was at the modal position, or conforming to the rest of the group. Schachter stated that this member allowed ''himself to be influenced step-by-step to the modal position,'' but did not instruct this soldier on how to reach conformity, only that prior to the end of the experiment, conformity was required. If the group's consensus shifted, the mode shifted as well. Through the experiment, Schacter wanted to see how group dynamics would influence or pressure a "deviant" role to conform.

The results of the experiment found that the "mode" soldier and the "slider" solider either followed the consensus of the group throughout the experiment or initially followed the "deviant" soldier, only to later conform to the group dynamics. Schachter's study found that over time, participants attempted to achieve conformity by increasing the amount of communication toward the "deviant" soldier. Once the group concluded that the "deviant" would not change or conform, the group would eventually cease to communicate with the "deviant" soldier. Additionally, as time progressed, group dynamics isolated the "deviant" soldier, who would eventually find him or herself being "left behind."

Within this group dynamic, as observed within Schacter's study, the role you subconsciously or consciously establish as your Hidden You will yield a group interaction of being inclusive or exclusive, and based on the amount of existing disruption within the group dynamics, you could be both for a period of time. This interaction and group dynamic is both subconsciously and consciously derived over time, and via our inborn self-preservation, will lead to either group acceptance or group isolation. As we observed in Chapter 4, the results of the infant study showed that even nonverbal six-month-old infants consider an individual's actions toward others when determining whether those actions are appealing, aversive, or self-preserving.

Your ability to influence will be highly dependent upon whether you are inclusive or exclusive within the group dynamics. When inclusive, group dynamics are supportive of new ideas or ideas that may be perceived to be nonconforming. In contrast, when you are exclusive, group dynamics are nonsupportive of new ideas and approaches, and nonconforming ideas are met with resistance, as such ideas are perceived to be detrimental to the group's self-preservation. When exclusive, as Schacter's study demonstrated, communication within the group diminishes and the deviant is rejected and "left behind." Any member of the group that feels exclusive or rejected, gone unnoticed, will only create unwanted social behaviors within the group dynamics, thereby adding another level of complexity.

As an influenceable star follower, establishing common nomenclature is an important concept to apply to group dynamics. Just as you will leverage the systematic approach of "move," "adapt," and "left behind" to assess and identify your progress to transcendent leadership, this same nomenclature will facilitate your ability to influence the group through enhanced communication. By establishing group nomenclature, as an individual or as a collective whole within a group, the ability to assess and discuss appropriate next steps based on the need to "move," "adapt," or be "left behind" is essential to one's ability to be influenceable and to lead transcendently.

To reach leadership transcendence and effectively "adapt," you must also master the instrumental qualities of enhanced communication beyond the three tenets discussed in this chapter.

CHAPTER 9

INSTRUMENTAL QUALITIES OF ENHANCED COMMUNICATION

> *Try not to become a man of success, but rather try to become a man of value.*
>
> —Albert Einstein

As part of your leadership evolution and systematic approach to leadership transcendence, this chapter will focus on the core components of the instrumental qualities of enhanced communication: listening, confronting reality, connecting, and inspiring.

To be an effective communicator, you must first learn how to listen. Easier said than done. This is without question one of the more challenging qualities to master. But to be a transcendent leader, you must learn how to listen, identify, and apply various forms of human psychology on those you intend to lead and help preserve.

For anyone who has visited a doctor or a psychiatrist, or seen one portrayed on television or in the movies, the first thing a doctor or psychiatrist does with a patient is sit them down and apply this extremely important technique called LISTENING. Before a doctor or a psychiatrist can administer any level of expertise, they must first ask strategic questions in order to listen, and hopefully capture key observations that will facilitate their ability to recommend or apply a remedy.

The most common disruptor of a leader's ability to "adapt" is directly correlated to a leader's inability to listen. A driving force behind this inability to listen is often associated with inborn human reactions to fear and in the caring and feeding for your own self-preservation. It is not uncommon for a leader to experience nervousness when conducting an interview or the first one-on-one to encourage relationship building, or of greater significance, the need to confront or correct a follower's inappropriate social behavior. Anyone in a leadership or a managerial role remembers the first hard conversation they had to have with an employee. In my case, it was a defining moment that represented the beginning of my own leadership evolution.

Having little to no management experience, and no mentor with significant leadership experience, I approached the first hard conversation with little to no discipline, and I clearly lacked any form of leadership transcendence. The approach consisted of reviewing and rehearsing how and what needed to be communicated. Breathing techniques learned in college to suppress the anxiety felt while doing activities such as public speaking were certainly applied. Throughout that day, all the way up to the actual one-on-one discussion, my limbic system and cerebral analysis were in constant conflict. My inherent fear, my inborn self-preservation, was invoking various chemical and electrical impulses throughout my entire body.

After what seemed a lifetime, I was ready to begin the one-on-one discussion. Just as rehearsed, I was ready to apply the communication I had rehearsed in my mind over and over. No small talk, no breaking the ice. I immediately outlined the information I had collected through proper inspection.

A fly on the wall would have described my applied communication as something like this: "TALK, TALK, TALK . . . TALK, TALK, TALK . . . TALK, TALK, TALK." This nonstop, one-way communication went on for the first ten minutes, until the individual I was seeking to influence vehemently interrupted me. The same fly on the wall would describe it as something like this: "LISTEN MAN, IF YOU WOULD SHUT THE HELL UP AND LET ME EXPLAIN THE SITUATION . . . !" Oh boy! Not the way you want your first challenging discussion to go. Total shock! At this point, my limbic system and cerebral analysis were in complete disarray, a level of confusion I had not experienced before. I don't think I said much more after that. After being forced to first listen, the only thing I can recall saying was, "I will do some more due diligence and we will pick up our discussion where we left off later." You might observe such a confrontation as insubordination, but in reality, it was my lack of maturity and understanding of leadership evolution, and my lack of a systematic approach to transcendent leadership, that was to blame for a bad, unprofessional form of communication. It was ultimately my inability to listen that led to this type of failed interaction.

I walked away from the experience embarrassed and confused. What had I done wrong? More importantly, I needed to understand how to avoid this situation in the future. In the world of leadership, you do not get to bestow upon yourself the title of leader. Even when group dynamics facilitate an acknowledgment of such qualities, it still does not qualify you as a leader. A leader must not only learn to listen to others, but they also must learn to listen to their instincts. We are all capable of making the right decision this way. Our instincts become more relevant to our ability to listen and make good decisions as we "move" and as we "adapt."

In Malcolm Gladwell's book *Blink: The Power of Thinking Without Thinking*, he describes how the consumption of information, in combination with long-term experience, facilitates our ability to make good decisions based on trusting our internal instincts. Malcolm describes a story where the J. Paul Getty Museum in California was seeking experts to determine the authenticity of a statue known as the Getty kouros (Gladwell, *Blink*, 2005). The Getty kouros is a life-size statue in the form of a late archaic Greek kouros. With a $9 million purchase at stake, the Getty Museum brought in several experts to examine the statue and validate its authenticity. Following examination, several experts were not convinced the statue was authentic. With no substantial proof, these experts could only draw upon their instincts that something was not right.

Regardless of their intuition, the dolomitic marble sculpture was bought by the J. Paul Getty Museum of Los Angeles, California, in 1985 and exhibited in October 1986 (Thomas, 1997). The significance of this purchase was that common scientific techniques, such as carbon dating, were used to validate the statue's approximate age. Although the carbon-dating results would indicate that the statue dated back to the appropriate timeframe, the experts were still not convinced.

It was only after the J. Paul Getty Museum purchased the piece that it was later determined to have a high probability of being fraudulent. To this day, many experts are still unconvinced that the kouros is an authentic piece of history, and the museum title in front of the statue describes a statue that either dates to about 530 BC or is a modern forgery. Regardless, you can recognize how through "move" and "adapt" concepts the experts were able to listen to their subconscious and conscious instincts, reflecting on a vast amount of experience and knowledge to make educated decisions, leading to a conclusion that facilitated their overall decision-making process.

In 1992, through meta-analysis, Nalini Ambady and Robert Rosenthal described this ability as "thin-slicing," a term within both psychology and philosophy that leverages social psychology and our adaptive subconscious instincts to articulate how we consume information over a period of time ("move") and how this facilitates our ability to make quick decisions (Ambady and Rosenthal, 1992). The term "thin slice" refers to the process of making quick inferences about the state, characteristics, or details of an individual or situation while only having a minimal amount of information (Wikipedia, Thin-slicing, n.d.). Judgments and decisions made through thin-slicing have been shown to be as accurate as those made when more information is available.

Given the dynamics that thin-slicing attributes to social behaviors, listening both to yourself and others will lead to greater transcendence as a leader. In a research paper published in 2007 by Dana R. Carney et al., it was concluded that first impressions have a greater chance for a positive encounter the wider the slice, or the longer two individuals are exposed to one another's information sharing process (Carney, Colvin, and Hall, 2007). Additionally, the wider the slice, the more information that can be shared, allowing for individuals to make more accurate judgments about each other's intentions. Dana et al. also drew the conclusion that women tended to make more accurate judgments with thin-slicing than men. This would make sense, as women have instincts that facilitate their ability to be better listeners.

A team from Cambridge University found key differences between the brains of men and women (Ruigrok, et al., 2013). Through this study, they concluded that women and men have variances in their limbic system and cerebral analysis process that lead to different forms of communication to satisfy their self-preservation. Amber Ruigrok, who carried out the study as part of her PhD, said, "For the first time we can look across the vast literature and confirm that brain size and structure are different in males and females. We should no longer ignore sex in neuroscience research, especially when investigating psychiatric conditions that are more prevalent in either males or females" (University of Cambridge, 2014). Therefore, we can conclude that the ability to recognize Hidden You concepts that facilitate effective thin-slicing dynamics associated with listening to your instincts, as well as the ability to more effectively listen to others, is essential to the leadership evolution and the systematic approach to transcendent leadership.

It's through the recognition and importance of first being a good listener that the process toward "adapting" facilitates the ability to address the next instrumental quality of enhanced communication: confronting reality. Before you can apply leadership transcendence to the systematic approach of "adapt," you must learn to confront reality. Learning how to confront reality is critical to your leadership evolution and your ability to lead transcendentally.

Through our inborn self-preservation, when things do not go the way we would have liked or intended, we want to believe things will return to normal, that there is an opportunity to have things as they were before. However, rarely is that ever the case. In order to confront reality, your Hidden You analysis and your ability to confront your behavioral instincts are the first steps needed to confront reality through transcendence. By assessing your and others' Hidden You, you can better leverage information to draw upon a realistic assessment to effectively "adapt" to any circumstance or situation. The real challenge in confronting reality is in your progress of "move" and your ability to successfully or even adequately dissect others' Hidden You—clearly not an easy task. However, through the discipline of time and perpetual preparation, it is achievable.

As a transcendent leader, confronting reality starts by disseminating the common nomenclature associated with "move," "adapt," and "left behind." This is essential to the facilitation of group dynamics and the group's ability to respond in unison, using a common group language or communication system, to collectively capture all the complexities an intended outcome requires, and to identify where in the systematic approach the group currently resides. You must use this common nomenclature to ask an individual or group pertinent questions that align to the systematic approach. Does the situation or circumstance require perpetual learning as a byproduct of "move," or does the group recognize that through listening and observation, the situation requires the group to "adapt" and to apply influence to reach an intended outcome? Or, through confronting reality, has the group been "left behind"? This is a topic we will explore in the next section.

As a transcendent leader, confronting reality and being honest with those you lead facilitates your ability to obtain good and realistic information from your followers. Leaders without Hidden You analysis subconsciously only want to hear what they want, information convenient to their inborn fears and personal self-preservation. Over time, without common nomenclature to facilitate the need to confront reality, followers become fearful of providing any information the leader has subconsciously—or sometimes deliberately—determined that they do not want to hear. It is through the systematic approach of "move," "adapt," or "left behind" that a leader can confront reality to ensure the group is committed to achieving intended outcomes, while at the same time not introducing group dynamics that prevent the group from confronting reality in order to "adapt" when adapting is required in order to not be "left behind."

Having spent the majority of my career within the information-technology industry, there is no better example of where the inability to confront reality has had a profound, even catastrophic impact on the vitality of many companies in this space.

Much too often, leaders turn to their own fears and inborn need for self-preservation and, as nontranscendent leaders, allow their subconscious to drive their social behavior and consequential group dynamics. Instead of being honest with their followers, they try to care for their perceived fears and self-preservation. This leads to an environment that does not confront reality, where social behaviors and unintended consequences prevail, and where intended outcomes get "left behind."

A great example of not confronting reality is when companies apply techniques such as removing the perceived "bottom 10 percent" performers from the business on an annual basis. Or when companies, often associated with appeasing shareholders, are forced to do mass layoffs via reduction in force measures. Without common nomenclature to confront reality through honesty and integrity, without a way to align the group to current situations and circumstance, overall group dynamics yield an environment where the survival of the fittest prevails. Individual subconscious self-preservation dominates, and leaders lack or are unable to obtain the information necessary to confront reality, which ultimately, through self-preservation, led them to make unrealistic promises. They slowly destroy the culture via a runaway group dynamic where bad social behaviors ultimately destroy the group and often create a death spiral within the business.

In order to prevent such catastrophic group dynamics and social behaviors, a leader must also learn how to connect. As we explored in Chapter 2: Survival Instincts, as humans we are predisposed through primal survival instincts to react to certain situations and events in a way that helps to ensure our overall self-preservation. To care for this instinctive self-preservation, we seek out certainty and comfort through the people we interact with. As we now recognize, not being accepted by the group or clan could have led to death. Within this inborn need to be part of a group, there also exists the need to connect, a way to find and maintain common ground with others. It is through our ability to connect that we find comfort in our desire for self-preservation.

In order to truly connect and to lead transcendentally, you must connect with all your followers—each individual. Now that does not necessarily mean that a leader of a large organization needs to personally connect with each individual; that is not realistic. However, through the systematic approach to leadership transcendence, a transcendent leader connects with their followers by consistently and successfully applying the instrumental qualities of enhanced communication. Through this application, a transcendent leader leads a group toward an intended outcome that, through common nomenclature, is easily understood and that facilitates a group dynamic where followers feel connected to the process of achieving intended outcomes.

When given the opportunity to connect at the individual level, it is through curiosity and "move" concepts that a transcendent leader can connect. By taking the time to listen and relate at an individual level, you will facilitate an overall group dynamic that seeks to care for the self-preservation of all.

To connect with others, there also exists the need to build or shape some form of likability. And given our human instinct and fear of rejection, who doesn't want to be liked? As we discovered, it is our Hidden You that helps determine our likability and the subsequent ability to connect with others. In the spirit of "move," learning how to "adapt" your Hidden You to facilitate likability is a skill. Some have an inborn or instinctive Hidden You that naturally drives a strong sense of likability. However, some do not have this natural aura and must learn to develop it. This is an essential skill.

Likability is an effective tool for driving intended social behavior and group dynamics toward intended outcomes and overall performance. In a study conducted by Jack Zenger, CEO of Zenger/Folkman, a strengths-based leadership development firm, he studied 51,836 leaders to determine their likability. Through his study, Zenger identified 27 leaders who were rated at the "bottom quartile in likability but were in the top quartile for overall leadership effectiveness" (Zenger, 2013). The results of the study concluded that 1 in 2,000 unlikable leaders are considered effective, a representation of the covariation model or groupthink, the former being concerned with both social perception and self-perception, and the latter leading to a perception that does not necessarily confront reality.

In an article written by Travis Bradberry of *Entrepreneur*, Travis identifies common attributes that can lead to being unlikable and eventual leadership isolation (Bradberry, 2016). All of these attributes are essential to avoiding the "Generation Now" social behaviors and self-inflicted anxiety and fear. The first attribute is what Travis describes as humble bragging, a form of communication that invokes subconscious levels of deception, which over time, through self-preservation instincts, causes the receiver to see right through the act of self-deprecation. As per the implicit personality theory or the covariation model, individuals who invoke humble bragging risk alienating themselves.

Travis's second attribute toward being unlikable is "being too serious." An association with someone who is always too serious can provoke a subconscious fear and anxiety within the social behaviors of those they interact with. As an alternative, being associated with someone who is serious and passionate when necessary but who is also open to having a balance of fun has a more positive impact on overall group dynamics.

Researchers at California's Loma Linda University constructed a study in hopes of better understanding how humor can deliver more than just comic relief (Federation of American Societies for Experimental Biology, 2014). Their study consisted of twenty healthy older adults, all between the ages of sixty and seventy, with the intent of using laughter to measure the potential impact on stress levels and short-term memory. The first group was asked to sit silently. The second group was presented funny videos. After twenty minutes, the participants within each group were asked to give saliva samples and were also given a short memory test. The study found that participants who viewed the funny videos scored higher on the short-term memory test. Of greater significance, the group that was introduced to humor showed considerably lower levels of cortisol, the stress hormone explored in Chapter 2: Survival Instincts.

It is human nature for people to gravitate toward those who are passionate, as absorbing their confidence subconsciously cares for your own self-preservation. However, it is just as easy for passionate people to be too passionate, which can lead to social behaviors that question your true interest and others' self-preservation versus your own. Travis states that "Likeable people balance their passion for their work with their ability to have fun. At work they are serious, yet friendly" (Bradberry, 2016). Leaders who are likable can get things accomplished while also finding time to be socially effective by capitalizing on valuable opportunities to connect with others without self-serving ambition. Through strong listening skills and sincerity, remembering and reminding others of past conversations demonstrates a connection that goes beyond the tenets of work. It is good for the instinctive self-preservation when past communications are acknowledged through demonstrated listening skills. Understanding this instrumental quality of enhanced communication is essential to being able to lead transcendentally.

Another critical attribute Travis associates with likability is emotional stability. Too often, the subconscious self-preservation and fear of failure gets the best of many leaders. Leaders, who carry an emotional burden, can never show emotional instability—not even once. As soon as a leader shows any level of instability, social behavior and group dynamics will question whether that leader is trustworthy and capable of keeping it together when it counts the most.

I learned this lesson the hard way. Prior to meeting with a client, I was part of a team where I took the lead in proactively mapping out the agenda for an upcoming face-to-face meeting. At the end of our mapping session, we all agreed on the agenda and next steps. Once in front of the customer, the team members who were expected to lead the discussion had made significant changes to the agenda without communicating such changes occurred. I was one of the uninformed. As a result, our team stumbled in front of this customer and we left with the perception of not being very organized and being very misaligned.

After the meeting ended, I confronted the individuals who changed the agenda without notifying the rest of the team. Although my communication in that moment was not too far out of bounds, my frustration was clear. I let fear and self-preservation get the best of me that day, and my communication style was less than becoming. As a result, I inadvertently demonstrated emotional instability and clearly lacked humbleness and an ability to inspire.

Followers seek out leaders who inspire, leaders who, regardless of the situation, show resolve and a "can-do attitude"—leaders who see issues or challenges as opportunity. Within the instrumental qualities of enhanced communication, inspiring others creates energy and motivation within those you lead. It helps form the culture that transcendent leaders are concerned with the self-preservation for all. This culture helps to influence group dynamics and how members will perceive each other and the many experiences along the way. As we explored within the Hidden You, leadership transcendence is about how to effectively communicate and create success by successfully managing a multitude of unknown failures. Failure can have a profoundly negative impact on the emotions and attitudes associated with group dynamics.

To counter our subconscious focus on the fear of failure, leaders must leverage inspiration to invoke contagious positive energy. Through inspiration, transcendent leaders communicate with authenticity and passion by first listening, confronting reality, and then connecting with their followers to care for the self-preservation desired by all and to ensure no one feels they are being "left behind."

Scott Barry Kaufman is the scientific director of the Imagination Institute in the Positive Psychology Center at the University of Pennsylvania. In an article he wrote for the *Harvard Business Review* titled "Why Inspiration Matters," Scott describes inspiration as that which "awakens us to new possibilities by allowing us to transcend our ordinary experiences and limitations. Inspiration propels a person from apathy to possibility, and transforms the way we perceive our own capabilities" (Kaufman, 2011). Scott goes on to describe inspiration as having three main qualities: evocation, transcendence, and approach motivation. First, inspiration is authentic, spontaneous, and evoked without intention. Second, inspiration is transcendent of our innate desire for self-preservation. Finally, inspiration involves approach motivation, where the individual, through instrumental qualities of enhanced communication, can creatively express or actualize a new idea or vision.

Within group dynamics, inspiration is vital to the caring and feeding of the social evaluation process. Exposing individuals or groups to inspiring leaders initiates needed creativity, and the ability to "adapt" to the pace at which things are changing in today's business climate. As Gregory Dess and Joseph Picken address in their article "Changing Roles: Leadership In the 21st Century," the global economy requires leaders to shift their attention from efficient management to effective delegation that utilizes the diversity of a company's available resources (Dess and Picken, 2000). In their article, they identify five key leadership roles:

1. "Using strategic vision to motivate and inspire." An accumulation of the next four key leadership roles. With these roles combined, a leader has the motivation and support to articulate the message, confront reality, and inspire followers to achieving desired outcomes.
2. "Empowering employees at all levels." Followers feel confident in taking action and making decisions within defined parameters. This provides a sense of ownership and pride.
3. "Accumulating and sharing internal knowledge." The ability to build a culture of trust. Information is provided freely and without judgment. The information given to leadership is based on what they need to hear, not what they want to hear.

4. "Gathering and integrating external information." The establishment of a culture where competitive analyses and market-trend analysis, another form of confronting reality, facilitate the ability to "move" and "adapt" within the required parameters.
5. "Challenging the status quo and enabling creativity." The establishment of a cultural social-evaluation process within the organization that is open to creativity. Creativity and open dialog is directly attributable to individual and group acceptance, and is vital to the self-preservation of all.

Transcendent leaders must be able to "adapt" to situations and circumstances on a consistent basis. While confronting reality, transcendent leaders must be able to evoke positive motivation that unleashes the creativity required for an individual or group to effectively influence and "adapt" to various circumstances and events in a way that provides for the caring, feeding, and self-preservation of all.

LEFT BEHIND

Just as a snake sheds its skin, we must shed our past over and over again.

— Gautama Buddha

In today's society and the world of leadership, we are continuously bombarded with self-help inspirational material that seeks to paint a utopian state where all the complexities we have explored thus far miraculously do not exist, or at a minimum are not being addressed within the framework of the social behaviors and networks we have explored.

Through our innate desire for acceptance, our craving for pleasure over fear, much of the available material seeks to inspire an interaction that feels good, but in reality is not realistic or practical, often leaving us feeling empty or confused. At a high level, most leadership self-help material, when simplified, has good intentions and, in a perfect world, would be of great significance. For example, creating a collaborative climate and encouraging open dialogue are worthy causes. Being inspired to build strong team mentalities and to recruit and nurture the highest-quality team members are excellent approaches. Through this form of leadership enlightenment, leaders are highly encouraged to be transparent and engage in healthy conflict through constructive confrontation, while also creating opportunities to receive honest and open feedback. Leaders are encouraged to confront and solve challenging situations with tact and diplomacy, while consistently demonstrating unwavering integrity, authenticity, and transcendence through compelling styles of communication.

As a leader, you are told to act empowered based on strong ownership and personal accountability, to hold high standards for yourself and others. You are encouraged to be bold, to go "against the grain" and to take informed risks. You are expected to be a relentless innovator, generating bold solutions while stimulating creativity.

The above is just a sampling of the messaging leaders will often receive. Through our Hidden You analysis and the systematic approach to leadership transcendence, it does not take a rocket scientist to recognize that this inspired form of leadership does not confront the reality of the many complex social behaviors and group dynamics we have explored. In fact, while on the surface this advice may seem practical and helpful, in reality, without a solid leadership foundation, it will only hasten the outcome of being "left behind."

I suspect many of us can recall when we first experienced the raw emotion of feeling left behind. Perhaps it was while shopping with our parents in a retail store and hiding in the clothing racks, only to discover you lost track of your parents. Maybe it was at a grocery store or a large amusement park and losing sight of those responsible for us invoked a fear of being left behind. Another example might be when a group of friends or colleagues did not invite you out, and by being excluded you felt left behind. In extreme cases, perhaps it was when your company decided they no longer needed your services and let you go. Regardless of the situation, it was in that moment of feeling left behind that triggered our fight-or-flight response. In each of those scenarios, whether through our survival instincts or learned social behaviors, we all have come to recognize being left behind as a negative event to be avoided whenever possible.

At the surface, the concept of "left behind" appears negative. However, what if I told you it was not bad at all—that perhaps being "left behind" is actually needed to become a transcendent leader? Society and many experts, including myself, believe that you must fail before you succeed. However, any form of failure, when experienced as an unintended consequence of doing the right thing, can and will have implications that reach beyond your own self-preservation. This is a conundrum, one that all leaders inherently face. It's almost as if the propensity for failure is inevitable. That's because it is!

As humans, there is an instinctive struggle within us between knowing when to follow and when to be independent. In essence, we are self-prescribing ourselves as our own self-subscribed leader in that moment. It is when our self-preservation is in jeopardy that we apply an internal hierarchy within ourselves, making ourselves the ultimate decision-maker that represents leadership independence, where we can put our faith in our own hands.

It is in these moments that an inborn rite of passage occurs, where your inherent desire to be an independent thinker is embraced and encouraged. As leaders, this rite of passage is backed by an authority to make decisions for followers who are either influencers or influenceable. What gets lost in translation is the fact that every decision invariably creates a set of consequences that can lead to a conflict with an individual or within existing group dynamics, thus igniting your instinctive fears. It's inevitable; it's a fact of life. Anyone without these instinctive attributes either has misfiring neurons, or they have come to recognize and balance their own fears. Regardless, the decisions you make will either get you closer to your desired outcome, or your decisions will get you farther away or potentially "left behind."

To be a transcendent leader, you must embrace the fact that you will get "left behind." Not once, not twice, but an infinite amount of times throughout your leadership evolution. Prior to reading this book, you might not have considered the consequences of making such decisions. However, when it comes to leadership transcendence, it is essential to understand that every decision you make will either bring you closer or further away from your intended outcome. You must recognize that the right decision may not lead to the best outcome, and the wrong decision can lead to a better outcome. Through Hidden You analysis and this systematic approach, you can at least be better positioned to make more optimal decisions that care for your innate fears while also caring for the self-preservation for all.

As Buddha so eloquently stated, "Just as a snake sheds its skin, we must shed our past over and over again." Failure is not an option, but it is inevitable. Through leadership transcendence, you will create a group dynamic that is relentless in pursuing facts and confronting reality. Through this systematic approach, no longer will unintended outcomes be one-dimensional with nowhere to go. Through the application of common nomenclature, an endless array of possibilities will present themselves.

Now, as much as the previous paragraph was intended to inspire, once again we must confront reality. The remaining chapters are intended to provide visibility into some of the more common experiences and attributes associated with being "left behind." To achieve leadership transcendence, you must recognize these attributes, embrace them, and through the systematic approach, grow as a result.

CHAPTER 10

SILOS, TURF WARS, AND LEADERSHIP ISOLATION

If your opponent is secure at all points, be prepared for him. If he is in superior strength, evade him. If your opponent is temperamental, seek to irritate him. Pretend to be weak, that he may grow arrogant. If he is taking his ease, give him no rest. If his forces are united, separate them. If sovereign and subject are in accord, put division between them. Attack him where he is unprepared, appear where you are not expected.

—Sun Tzu's *The Art of War*

Through the complexities of group dynamics and the social behaviors associated with the variations found amongst the Hidden You in society, it's not hard to conceptualize how easy it is for silos and turf wars to manifest themselves within cultures, family systems, and organizations— where the self-preservation of a few is in conflict with the self-preservation of many. By not addressing silos and turf wars, a leader is more susceptible to leadership isolation and the subsequent social behaviors by individuals and groups that seek to disrupt the existing hierarchy or decision-making process. Unfortunately, this predictable anomaly exists everywhere, often manifesting itself when one group's self-preservation is at risk and groupthink determines it can provide a certain function or outcome more effectively than another group. Without defined lines of role and responsibility associated with one group versus another, silos and turf wars are free to manifest, slowly wreaking havoc on an organization or business's ability to meet intended outcomes.

Silos are created when group dynamics and the need for group self-preservation create invisible barriers that isolate a group from wanting to contribute to the broader success of an organization or higher purpose in fear of being "left behind." The social dynamics associated with silos have no bias in terms of place or time. In society, they are often driven by such "things" as religious sovereignty, human conflict in association with perceived birth rights, or self-anointed experts. At work, they are often created when two groups provide similar functions, and the need to outshine the other group subconsciously resonates and overtime becomes an unspoken objective of the group dynamic.

Similar to silos, turf wars are where group dynamics and the need for group self-preservation not only isolate a group from wanting to share and contribute to the broader success of an organization or higher purpose, but the fear of losing control and subsequently being "left behind" causes the group to protect its turf. These groups protect their perceived ownership by taking extreme measures of isolation, while openly communicating the need to defend their position at all costs. Turf wars are often associated with a form of conflict and society's need to relinquish or take control of something from another. At work, a turf war is often associated with two organizations performing the same function, and through consolidation, only one will maintain control going forward. History is splattered with examples associated with socioeconomics, where the economic well-being of many is disrupted or in conflict with the economic well-being of others, leading to the existence of both a silo and a turf war.

Silos and turf wars commonly manifest themselves within large organizations or corporations in the form of "office politics."

Prior to "office politics," multiple organizations or lines of business were established or built with the intention of working together for a common purpose or goal and in pursuit of ensuring the self-preservation for all. When it comes to silos and turf wars, conflict prevails, and organizations end up competing and working against each other, consciously and subconsciously, starving and depriving each other from obtaining mutual success.

What's the number-one culprit for the existence of silos and turf wars? Bad leadership, for sure! With a world that is void of transcendent leaders, you should and can expect to be confronted by and to work within various forms of silos and turf wars. However, truth be told, even when leadership transcendence is present, the chance for silos and turf wars to develop is still highly probable, almost guaranteed. It is therefore a transcendent leader's responsibility to stay diligent, constantly observing and seeking out the existence or formation of such conflicts to help prevent them from occurring and disrupting the self-preservation of all. In doing so, it is equally important for transcendent leaders to recognize the potential for creating leadership isolation.

As an active member of society, we are all expected to contribute, which often facilitates our contributions to silos and turf wars. Through our contributions, our need for acceptance invokes a conscious and subconscious desire to bear fruit, to achieve acceptance that cares for our self-preservation within a segment of society, and then to protect it. Through fear of rejection and the need for acceptance, you inevitably expose yourself to the diversity of society and to the complexities of the Hidden You, which enhances the desire to protect what you have worked so hard to achieve.

As a transcendent leader, you are exposed to unique individuals and complex group dynamics, where your experience and knowledge will influence decisions, circumstances, and outcomes that can yield both positive and negative reactions. The more you experience negative events or forms of failure, the more you gain visibility into society's diversity, and the more you come to recognize and understand the complexities associated with the various cultures and social behaviors that are invoked to sustain self-preservation.

As a result, through your own self-preservation, you think more critically and intuitively about the many events and circumstances you have experienced, consciously and subconsciously seeking to better understand human nature and how to overcome its many unforeseen and incomprehensible challenges. You explore ways to better understand what drives and motivates the overall decision-making process, which conjures up an inborn desire to better understand the full intentions of those you interact with on a daily basis.

Due to the need for acceptance, when it comes to silos and turf wars, influenceable group members who are willing to compromise their overall self-preservation through trusting another's leadership will invariably find themselves under the guidance or direction of others. They will often be forced to focus on what other people want and expect, even though their instincts are conveying that an alternative approach may be required. This is an environment where it's easy to fall into a trap where everything they do is for the benefit of a select few and not for the greater whole. They are consumed in making sure they are looked upon favorably by the select few who are perceived to be in power and hold their self-preservation in their hands.

To minimize your exposure to silos and turf wars, you must take responsibility for your Hidden You and recognize the inherent social behaviors associated with these conflicts. Through the merits of leadership psychology, you must be accountable and purposeful in your ability to "move" and "adapt" by using your influence to drive a universally beneficial outcome.

As a transcendent leader, you cannot ignore that the majority of society is not interested, and will never fully understand nor see the need for pursuing a leadership evolution. As Winston Churchill so elegantly stated, "The truth is incontrovertible. Panic may resent it, ignorance may deride it, malice may distort it, but there it is" (Speech in the House of Commons, 1916). Whether it is panic, malice, or ignorance, history has provided many life lessons for aspiring transcendent leaders to learn and grow from in their activities.

In the world of silos, turf wars, and subsequent office politics, certain subconscious and conscious social behaviors can be observed. Books like Sun Tzu's *The Art of War* or Robert Greene's *48 Laws of Power* confront reality while also providing tremendous knowledge and insight into the type of destructive human social behaviors that seek power and hierarchy, while also leaving a path of devastation and leadership isolation for those in charge. Having a basic understanding of these inborn behaviors, where self-preservation drives a behavior steeped in dishonesty, deceit, and ill will, is essential to becoming a transcendent leader. When backed into a corner, humans have time and time again shown an ability to make questionable and inappropriate decisions that can negatively impact a wide population while minimizing the impact to an individual or a small segment of the population.

What is it about this inherent human desire to be at the top of the hierarchy? Is it truly a desire for acceptance, or is it an innate fear of rejection? In reality, the answers to these questions do not truly matter. What matters is that regardless of how your Hidden You analysis addresses hierarchy, acceptance, and/or rejection, understanding the inborn instincts and subconscious pitfalls that lead to silos, turf wars, and ultimately leadership isolation are not to be taken lightly and must be confronted through historical observations.

The epigraph found at the beginning of this chapter, a quote from Sun Tzu's *The Art of War*, does an exceptional job of simplifying human instinct, both consciously and subconsciously, as it relates to dominating another, which often leads to leadership isolation. It depicts a strategy for achieving hierarchy and order with the intent to deceive and destroy when necessary, all to obtain ultimate power. As a transcendent leader, there will be times when the self-preservation for all requires you to be calculating, and you will need to influence with a specific purpose. The challenge is that there will always be a subconscious or conscious desire to also look out for your own self-preservation. It is only through Hidden You analysis, through your ability to "move" and "adapt," that you can ensure and enforce through proper cerebral analysis a decision-making process that perpetually seeks the self-preservation for all.

Regardless, you will be exposed to life's many challenges and the many social behaviors associated with those who seek power through their own inborn needs. As a transcendent leader or a transcendent follower, you must confront reality and recognize that it is extremely likely that over your career you will work for a "turkey," someone who has no leadership evolution. It is in these situations where the systematic approach of "move," "adapt," or "left behind" is critical to increasing your odds of successfully traversing such challenging environments.

As an exercise of enlightenment, we will examine each sentence of Sun Tzu's quote (Tzu and Giles, 2009). We will evaluate each sentence through the lens of a "turkey" and through the lens of a transcendent leader. The first two sentences state "If your opponent is secure at all points, be prepared for him. If he is in superior strength, evade him." A transcendent leader who is secure at all points is comfortable through their Hidden You analysis. You must be prepared for a transcendent leader, as they are ready to handle any situation through their transcendence. In preparation, a transcendent leader has confronted reality, established common nomenclature, and is able to capture real-time information from their followers. Any information that does not confront reality will not be underestimated by a transcendent leader, yet will be observed appropriately. If they determine the information is inaccurate, they will confront, seek clarity, and leverage the interaction as a teaching moment, thereby seeking future alignment between transcendent leader, follower, and even a "turkey."

For a "turkey," this sentence sets a different tone. A "turkey" has no Hidden You analysis to reflect upon. They are guarded and mindful of their perceived adversary's weakness, and look to exploit such weakness for their own benefit. A "turkey" is eager to impress, and will work overtime to capture the information needed. In capturing this information, a "turkey" will either use manipulation or deception, or when in a role of authority, fear and intimidation. "Turkeys" are calculating and have a conscious goal of moving up the hierarchy. They consciously seek power, as power brings them individual prestige.

Tzu's third and fourth sentence state, "If your opponent is temperamental, seek to irritate him. Pretend to be weak, that he may grow arrogant." A transcendent leader is not easily aroused and is nontemperamental. They will proactively embrace those with perceived weakness to turn that weakness into strength. Through common nomenclature, transcendent leaders will uncover strengths through addressing a follower's weakness. Transcendent leaders do not pretend by virtue of authentic or transcendence representation.

A "turkey" is quick to become irritated and temperamental, as they have no Hidden You analysis to reflect upon. "Turkeys" make great adversaries for each other, as they can exploit each other's weaknesses. It is the "turkey" who is consciously able to make another "turkey" irritable and temperamental, and together they are cyclical in their congruence of malice and ignorance alike.

Tzu's fifth and sixth sentences state, "If he is taking his ease, give him no rest. If his forces are united, separate them." As a transcendent leader, ease and rest are byproducts of transcendent leadership. That is not to insinuate that results associated with transcendent leadership are not being achieved. To the contrary, transcendent leaders build a culture of empowerment and collaboration. It is through this culture that a group of followers unite around their transcendent leader. The byproduct is substantial achievement through the assurance of self-preservation of all. For a "turkey," separating a transcendent leader's followers is difficult. Even in the circumstance where a transcendent leader and their followers are perceived to have failed, the followers will not separate. Through common nomenclature and the ability to effectively confront reality, they will simply assess the current state to reach a more amiable future state. It is only when a "turkey" seeks to overthrow another "turkey" that they are separated from their followers. "Turkeys" get no rest, as they are constantly under siege by other "turkeys."

Tzu's seventh and eighth sentences state, "If sovereign and subject are in accord, put division between them. Attack him where he is unprepared, appear where you are not expected." Transcendent leaders are inherently good followers. They seek conformity and alignment, not division. To "turkeys," transcendent leaders have a knack for appearing where they were not expected. The difference is that the unexpected appearance of a transcendent leader is not done with malice or ignorance; it occurs as a result of their ability to effectively "move" and "adapt" to lead authentically and through transcendence. For "turkeys," creating divide amongst other "turkeys" is not uncommon. Many leaders today have no leadership evolution and are often insecure. It is through this common attribute that "turkeys" wreak havoc amongst each other.

In Robert Greene's book *48 Laws of Power*, his first law states, "Never outshine your master" (Green, 1998). As the first law, it is the most important to understand. To outshine your master is to evoke their fear of self-preservation by creating a perception that you are better than them. True leaders—transcendent leaders—are focused on the self-preservation for all and will embrace the opportunity to be outshined by their followers. For any transcendent leader or follower who finds themselves under the leadership of someone who is unable to facilitate or allow their followers to outshine them, that leader will inevitably find themselves being "left behind." A leader under this scenario will spend more time prioritizing their self-preservation over the self-preservation of all. In leadership transcendence, you must "move," taking the time to learn from history and seeking greater knowledge regarding the social behaviors of those who, through malice or ignorance, disrupt your ability to reach leadership transcendence. In order to lead amongst the plethora of inexperienced leaders, you must understand them so you can "adapt" to their tactics and behaviors. It is through this understanding that a transcendent leader can better observe their surroundings and be better prepared to care for the self-preservation of those they have been given the opportunity to lead.

William Blake was an English poet, painter, and printmaker who once said, "He who pretends to be either painter or engraver without being a master of drawing is an imposter" (Wikipedia, n.d.). How can you be transcendent if you have not learned your Hidden You? How can you lead if you have no leadership foundation or systematic approach that facilitates common nomenclature in order to know when to "move" and "adapt"? The simple answer is you can't. Silos, turf wars, and leadership isolation will always exist in one form or another. It is unavoidable. It is through the lack of a leadership foundation or systematic approach that the implications imposed by immature leaders will permeate and create silos, turf wars, and leadership isolation for many.

As a transcendent leader, addressing such circumstance is imperative. A leader should evaluate across the business or within the organization where silos, turf wars, and leadership isolation might exist. Enacting this type of evaluation, a process that confronts reality, is critical to ensuring a healthy culture. Common nomenclature regarding silos, turf wars, and leadership isolation must exist amongst the group dynamics. One of the more effective ways to lessen the impact of a nontranscendent leader, or any attribute that seeks to diminish team success, is to identify, confront, and care for the type of social behaviors that lead to silos, turf wars, and leadership isolation. Being proactive and establishing a culture that enables the discussion of human social behaviors within existing group dynamics represents strong leadership transcendence.

No other book has sold more copies than the Bible, and no other book can provide as much wisdom regarding leadership transcendence (Guinness World Records, 2017). As an example, Philippians 2:2–4, Unity through Humility, states, "Let nothing be done through selfish ambition or conceit, but in lowliness of mind let each esteem others better than himself. Let each of you look out not only for his own interests, but also for the interests of others" (NKJV). Although silos, turf wars, and leadership isolation are in some ways a rite of passage in your leadership evolution, when it comes to leadership in general, the sooner you reach "self-transcendence," the sooner you reach a form of leadership that is an inspiration toward the self-preservation for all.

The process itself can create unexpected challenges along the way. Social behaviors that resonate instinctively within the population will expose leaders to situations and circumstances that are not only anticipated, but will question why anyone would step into a leadership role to begin with. In fact, most leaders do not choose their role; their role chooses them. Similar to having fifteen minutes of fame, at some point in time, everyone will have an opportunity to fulfill a leadership role. What you choose to do with such an opportunity is up to you. You can proactively prepare for such an opportunity, or do nothing at all.

A systematic approach to leadership transcendence can be a catalyst for preparing or enhancing your leadership skills and your ability to better understand and interact with society as a whole. Regardless of your role—leader or follower—you will be subjected to the same social dynamics associated with silos, turf wars, and leadership isolation. Through these dynamics, you will face the fear of rejection and failure. It is how you deal with such consequences, and the process for understanding and overcoming them, that you learn how to avoid being "left behind."

CHAPTER 11

FAILURE IS A FORM OF SUCCESS

> *Failure is only the opportunity to begin again more intelligently.*
>
> —Henry Ford

One of the greatest challenges we all face is our inability to accept or cope with failure. This is especially true when it comes to leadership. As a leader, one of the main tenets of leadership is the ability to successfully manage an individual or group through various forms of failure. A leader is expected to help an individual or group overcome failure to reach a successful outcome. For any leader, this is a heavy burden, and little attention is given to the inborn stress and anxiety they must face, especially given the "Generation Now" mentality and the overall obsession with failure.

Think about it. When was the last time you or the organization you represent spent any significant amount of time examining and reviewing success? If you are like most, the answer is never. Sure, most leaders might identify areas or components of success. Most will even acknowledge individuals or groups for achieving measurable goals. However, beyond acknowledgment, when is success actually examined, where root cause is clearly identified and not replaced with an alternative approach, but captured and replicated throughout the organization?

Why do our social behaviors drive so much attention toward understanding our failures? When it comes to our survival instincts and self-preservation, we are all wired with an innate desire and need to apply greater concentration on understanding and determining how to overcome our failures. After all, no one gets kicked out for being successful. At least, not in most cases.

In order to fully leverage this systematic approach to leadership transcendence and to embrace the concept of "left behind," you must come to recognize failure as a form of success. To do this, to be able to successfully learn and grow from failure, you need a systematic approach to effectively traverse the many physiological and psychological challenges that being "left behind" often creates. Through Hidden You knowledge as it relates to the human physiological reaction to both failure and fear, one you must learn to embrace your failures, as well as the natural psychological reaction that occurs when experiencing fear and rejection. As you appreciate and understand the nature of such reactions, you are able to consciously apply a form of cerebral analysis that facilitates an ability to manage and compartmentalize such fears.

An excellent component of society where you can observe "move," "adapt," and "left behind" through real-world analysis as it relates to failure as a form of success is in examining well-known military leaders. Historical review offers insight into the Hidden You, the leadership-evolution journey, and the decision-making process of those who were in significant leadership roles. History allows us to observe how society judged the effectiveness of such leaders.

In war, military leaders are subjected to realities that few leaders will ever have to address. What is referred to as "left behind" is represented by a more severe outcome, often in the form of death. Death is highly probable, and as a result, subconscious human instincts for self-preservation reach a heightened sensitivity within the mind and decision-making process of such leaders.

Through these dynamics, we can observe how Hidden You analysis impacts a leader's ability to make difficult decisions, where their decision can literally be the difference between life and death. Of greater intrigue is how, through these unique observations, we can apply Hidden You concepts and an outline of the systematic approach to leadership transcendence, allowing us insight into how our new Hidden You knowledge can be observed through this historical lens.

US Civil War (Sherman's March to the Sea)

During the United States Civil War, there were well-known generals who each represented different characteristics and attributes associated with the Hidden You and the systematic approach to leadership transcendence. Each bore unique strengths and weaknesses that impacted their ability to lead transcendently. Two of these generals were George B. McClellan and William Tecumseh Sherman, both of whom once held the highest position as general of the Union Army. One would go on to become general of the United States Army. Through the many challenges and failures they experienced up to and during their leadership roles in the Civil War, each experienced their own unique leadership journey.

Through examining these two leaders, we can observe their overall effectiveness, and how their Hidden You played a role in their successes and failures. We must also recognize that these leaders were not privy to the neuroscience studies and research provided via modern technology. Maslow and Murray, and the many other psychologists who contributed to leadership psychology, had not yet been born. Jung's personality theories were yet to be derived. McClellan and Sherman would experience the trials and tribulations associated with leadership at a time when leadership psychology was in great demand. Without such advanced knowledge, each could only rely on their own intuition. They would apply subconscious systematic approaches to their leadership journeys, each yielding different outcomes.

The first general we will cross examine is George Brinton McClellan, born in 1826 (Williams, 1991, p. 7). During his leadership journey, McClellan served in many different leadership roles. He served in the army more than once, having served in the US Army and then later in the Union Army. As a civilian, McClellan was a civil engineer, a railroad executive, and a politician. Of all his leadership roles, it was his role during the Civil War that would most define and ultimately expose his leadership attributes through the eyes of history.

General George Brinton McClellan (1826–1885)

McClellan had many inborn gifts, one of which was his extreme intellect. He was the third of five children born to Dr. George and Elizabeth (Brinton) McClellan. Although McClellan would fail at his future run for president of the United States, it is worth noting that fifty-two percent of our presidents have come from families where they have older and younger siblings (Schumann, 2011). In a blog written by Lynne Griffin, RN, EdM, where she interviews Katrin Schumann, coauthor of *The Secret Power of Middle Children*, Griffin asks, "How does growing up a middle child influence adult life, career, and relationships?"

Katrin answered, "Your family position relates to the jobs you're drawn to and how you interact with people in the workplace. Middles are flexible, team-builders, independent, yet also social. They don't need to be micromanaged. These are critical skills in the modern work world. They would make good teachers, actors, social workers, diplomats—but would not be so good at work where they're isolated (i.e., computer programmer) or when they have a position of authority in which they have to micromanage other people. Empathy can cause them stress—they'd make good defense lawyers, but not good prosecutors" (Griffin, 2012).

As we examine McClellan's early life and leadership career, portions of Katrin's observations will certainly become identifiable. However, like all of us, our Hidden You can take on several different characteristics that can reach across many different personalities and power personas. As we grow older and aspire for self-transcendence, the ability to cut across many different personalities and power personas to maximize effective communication is often inherent. Without self-transcendence, leaders often experience ineffective communication. It is not uncommon for nontranscendental leaders to dominate one category of personality and power persona, making effective communication and connection more difficult.

At thirteen years old, McClellan was already displaying a strong sense of curiosity. After attending the preparatory academy at the University of Pennsylvania, he entered the university to study law. After two years of studying, his curiosity continued to broaden. Finding himself disinterested in law, McClellan's curiosity led him down a different path toward military service. Taking advantage of his family system and their association with the upper ranks of Philadelphia society, McClellan was able to manipulate time and take a shortcut to success. When he was first left off the list of West Point nominees, his father, a prominent Philadelphia surgeon, wrote a letter to President of the United States John Tyler. Although never proven, it is believed by many historians that President Tyler would influence McClellan's acceptance into the United States Military Academy at West Point in 1842 (Sears, 1988, p. 3) (Rafuse, 2005, pp. 27–28). In order to fulfill this request and accept McClellan at fifteen years of age, the president would have to influence the academy to waive its normal minimum-age requirement of sixteen—a requirement that was not waived for just anyone.

For McClellan, instead of facing adversity, failure, or the need for patience, his self-preservation would be catered to through his family's influence. This was significant, representing an early moment in McClellan's life where the opportunity to experience adversity was replaced by his father's ability to manipulate the normal order of time.

McClellan's experience at West Point represented a significant contribution to his overall leadership journey. It was during this time that he was first introduced and captivated by battle tactics. While attending West Point, McClellan was able to "move," where he was first introduced to war history and the effectiveness of strategic wartime tactics. What is not easily observed through his time at West Point is how much of McClellan's "move" and curiosity was focused on the subject of leadership. Unlike today, there was little to no written work on the specifics of leadership. The curriculum at West Point was more focused on engineering and soldier attributes.

McClellan established early success at West Point, demonstrating an innate drive toward academic excellence, and at the age of twenty would go on to graduate second in his class of fifty-nine cadets. The only reason he was not first was due to demerits he had received as part of the disciplinary program. Following graduation, McClellan was commissioned as a brevet second lieutenant in the US Army Corps of Engineers and would receive his first orders, which required him to join the Mexican–American War (Eicher and J., 2001, p. 371). McClellan was tasked with performing several reconnaissance missions for Major General Winfield Scott, a close friend of his father, and who would become a future adversary to the younger, inexperienced McClellan (Rafuse, 2005, p. 43). An interesting circumstance, as Maj. Gen. Winfield Scott found favor in the young McClellan and provided tremendous support and influence in his future assignments and overall career within the army.

As a young lieutenant, McClellan was eager and needed recognition and acceptance. Through family and political influence, his high ambitions and strong will toward self-preservation were catered to during the early years of his leadership journey. He began to overindulge in the consumption of bull dung, a necessary dietary supplement for someone who wishes to cut corners.

During his extended time at West Point, McClellan and his corps of engineers were assigned to various expeditions to assist with land surveys to find new railroad routes for the secretary of war at the time, Jefferson Davis. Beginning in the 1840s, several government-sponsored expeditions were undertaken in hopes of discovering safe passage across the rugged terrain of the western United States. On March 3, 1853, Congress appropriated $150,000 authorizing Secretary of War Jefferson Davis "to ascertain the most practical and economical route for a railroad from the

Mississippi river to the Pacific Ocean" (Wikipedia, Pacific Railroad Surveya, n.d.).

Right place, right time, Jefferson Davis ordered Brevet Captain McClellan and his Corps of Topographical Engineers (TOPOGS), a new division in the United States Army ,to fulfill this obligation. It was during this time that Jefferson Davis found favor in McClellan's charming power persona. In March 1855, at the age of twenty-nine, Davis promoted McClellan to captain, assigning him to the 1st US Cavalry regiment (Eicher and J., 2001, p. 371). This was a significant moment in McClellan's leadership journey, allowing him to ascend to the next branch of leadership both in title and in responsibility. It had taken McClellan more than six years to go from second to first lieutenant, and he was promoted to captain in less than two years. Through various forms of communication uncovered from Jefferson Davis's archives, it was clear that Davis found favor in the young McClellan, but a leadership mentor he was not.

Through McClellan's extended family relationships and his blossoming political connections inside and outside the army, he would continue to find favor in his future assignments. Through his brother John's influence in Washington, DC, McClellan sought favor in the assignment of one of several commissions sponsored by Jefferson Davis (Sears, 1988, p. 44). In 1855, McClellan was commissioned and assigned as an official observer of war tactics, weaponry, and logistics for the Crimean War. As a nonparticipant of the European armies in the Crimean War, McClellan's curiosity and expanded knowledge of war tactics would thrive. This represented a significant contribution to his future leadership journey, as it facilitated his ability to observe war tactics while also interacting with the military's highest in command and the associated royal families. It was also during this time that history has recorded McClellan's inborn Hidden You weaknesses—insubordination and a lack of discipline. These weaknesses likely originated from a strong self-perception through his charming power persona, while also indulging in political bull dung via his family's influence.

Again finding himself in the right place at the right time, to seize on the financial opportunity afforded to him through his vast experience with the transcontinental railroad expeditions, on January 16, 1857, at the age of thirty-one, McClellan resigned his commission in the army to become chief engineer and eventually vice president of the Illinois Central Railroad—a remarkable accomplishment considering his career up to this point included little adversity with little to no failure. It was as vice president of the Illinois Central Railroad that McClellan would first meet the future President of the United States Abraham Lincoln.

Moving from a life of serving his country and into civilian life, McClellan did not ascend to a higher leadership branch. Instead, as a representation of leadership within civilian life, he moved to another branch of equal height. He found great success in civil employment, and through good timing, two years into his new line of work in the railroad industry, he accepted the position of president of the Ohio and Mississippi Railroad. In relation to the concept of "move" during his civilian employment, McClellan continued to feed his curiosity and obsession with military strategy, which would contribute to his ability to influence his future appointment as a military leader in the Union Army.

Over the years, as the realities and onset of the American Civil War emerged, McClellan leveraged his knowledge in war tactics and local politics to influence his role in the war. Through his tactical knowledge, he would successfully influence many of society's elites, positioning himself as someone who would excel at military leadership. Several aristocrats who, through their acquaintances with McClellan would consume his bull dung, came to believe in what truly amounted to untested leadership and war inexperience.

As a result of McClellan's influence, the governors of Ohio, Pennsylvania, and New York, the three largest states of the Union, actively pursued him to command their state's militia. McClellan, who had always had strong ambition for military leadership, on April 23, 1861, was commissioned by Ohio Governor William Dennison as a major general of volunteers, where McClellan took command of the Ohio militia. McClellan left civilian employment and moved back to his previous perch on the leadership branch associated with military service, where he had last served his country.

With the growing unrest associated with the Civil War, McClellan joined the Union Army. On May 3, 1861, McClellan ascended one branch higher and re-entered military service as commander of the Department of the Ohio, responsible for the defense of Ohio, Indiana, Illinois, and later, western Pennsylvania, western Virginia, and Missouri. Then on May 14 of that same year, through extreme acceleration, he ascended to the next leadership branch and was commissioned as major general in the regular army—without ever having to lead a group of men into battle.

At the young age of thirty-four, with little to no military leadership nor battle experience, he outranked everyone in the army except Lt. Gen. Winfield Scott, who, at the age of seventy-five, was now the general-in-chief of the Union Army. Unlike Lt. Gen. Winfield Scott's career, where Scott had successfully waged and won several battles, McClellan's rapid promotion was in large part due to his acquaintance and successful influential relationship with Salmon P. Chase (Sears, 1988, p. 72). Chase was the treasury secretary and a former Ohio governor and senator whose own influence would play a role in influencing others without inspecting McClellan's actual capabilities. Although McClellan had not quite reached the highest branch, he was getting close, and doing so in record time. It is also important to note that up to this point in McClellan's career, still no leadership mentor can be identified.

As part of McClellan's new leadership role, he oversaw the processing of several thousand men who were volunteering to serve in the Civil War. This required coordination and managerial logistics for setting up training camps. Of greater significance, it continued the progression of McClellan's curiosity, and for the first time in his career provided an opportunity for him to put this vast knowledge into practice. Only four days after assuming command in Ohio, McClellan wrote a letter to his late father's good friend, Lt. Gen. Winfield Scott, offering his unsolicited proposal for the Union strategy. In this proposal, he provided two alternatives to include a self-serving recommendation to promote him to commander. Although McClellan had a strong curiosity and an inherent desire to "move" in his knowledge of military strategy, his self-preservation, lack of Hidden You analysis, and inherent inability to be influenceable was on full display to Lt. Gen. Winfield Scott.

Lt. Gen. Winfield Scott, a man with considerable leadership and battle-tested experience, rejected both of McClellan's unsolicited plans, describing them as logistically unfeasible. In a moment of grace and potential transcendence as a leader, he complimented McClellan and expressed his "great confidence in [his] intelligence, zeal, science, and energy" (Sears, 1988, p. 76). Leveraging his vast military experience, Lt. Gen. Winfield Scott communicated in his response that the eighty thousand men, accompanied by a strong Union blockade of Southern ports, would be better used on a river-based expedition to control the Mississippi River and split the Confederacy.

Through historical observation, it is possible that McClellan had good intentions and meant no disrespect through his recommendation. Likewise, it is possible that Lt. Gen. Winfield Scott's own Hidden You did not facilitate an open environment, where outshining the master is met with subconscious bias. However, it is more likely that Lt. Gen. Winfield Scott's reaction was that of a transcendent leader. Through instrumental qualities of enhanced communication, Lt. Gen. Winfield Scott was open to McClellan's ideas, being careful not to discourage him from future communications. In review of McClellan's strategies, Lt. Gen. Winfield Scott applied subconscious "thin-slicing" techniques to evaluate his proposed strategies, while also confronting reality and seeking not to just care for the self-preservation of his good friend's son, but also considering the preservation of all.

Lt. Gen. Winfield Scott's war strategy and plan, which became known as the "Anaconda Plan," would require considerable patience, and in time would prove to be the outline for the Union's successful end to the Civil War. For McClellan, instead of "adapting" and finding ways to be a "star follower" to include leveraging his opportunity to influence through top-down, inside-out, and bottom-up leadership principles, McClellan chose a different path. He chose not to confront reality, he chose not to listen, and without any leadership foundation or systematic approach to draw upon, he became an "alienated follower" to his leader, Lt. Gen. Winfield Scott. As expected, in a relatively short period of time, the relations between the two generals became increasingly strained (Sears, 1988, pp. 75–76). Remarkably, in spite of the their strained relationship, McClellan found pockets of success through his ability to manage complex army logistics when training infantry and in his ability to connect with his troops through demonstrating his desire for their self-preservation.

As preparation for the war continued, McClellan's first military operations were to occupy the area of western Virginia that wanted to remain in the Union. McClellan demonstrated a propensity for doing exactly what Napoleon Hill would describe as leadership failure. He would manage with fear, keeping his intentions to himself in fear of conspiracy or attempts to see him fail. He consistently showed an inability to relegate details to capable lieutenants. Without star followers to delegate important tasks to, over time he was unable to avoid the traps of failure and was moving toward leadership isolation. To achieve successful outcomes on a consistent basis, a leader must have a systematic approach to incorporate common nomenclature that drives consistency in how they communicate. McClellan had none.

On May 26, 1861, McClellan had received reports that the critical Baltimore and Ohio railroad bridges were being burned by Confederate soldiers (Sears, 1988, pp. 78–79). As McClellan implemented plans to invade the region, once again, his inborn ambition and subconscious self-preservation got the better of him, resulting in his first serious political controversy. In complete disregard for military protocol, prior to engaging, McClellan proclaimed to the citizens of the region that his forces had no intentions of interfering with personal property, including their slaves. McClellan stated, "Notwithstanding all that has been said by the traitors to induce you to believe that our advent among you will be signalized by interference with your slaves, understand one thing clearly—not only will we abstain from all such interference, but we will on the contrary with an iron hand, crush any attempted insurrection on their part" (Sears, 1988, p. 79).

As word of McClellan's communication made its way through the Union ranks, McClellan's subconscious physiological reaction to fear likely intervened, and he realized he had overstepped his bounds. He immediately apologized by letter to President Abraham Lincoln. For McClellan, this oversight was not that his message opposed the administration's policy at the time, but that he had overstepped his authority beyond his clearly defined military role. McClellan was now demonstrating at the highest levels of the Union Army a significant void in leadership courtesy, while also continuing to display "alienated followership" toward leadership at the highest level.

Miraculously, McClellan overcame many of his inherent Hidden You weaknesses, as well as his lack of leadership skills, through his managerial and logistical skills that early in the war allowed his forces to move with great effectiveness. This would prove to be beneficial to his early perceived leadership skills in battle. Arguably the first land conflict of the Civil War, McClellan's first battle, the Battle of Philippi, was a small skirmish that would lay the foundation for his perception as a strong military leader—not because of the way he won the skirmish, but more to do with "timing" and his force's ability to outmaneuver a young and inexperienced Confederate Army.

In McClellan's second confrontation with the Confederate Army, he would once again outmaneuver the enemy. Representing his first personal commanding win in battle, the Battle of Rich Mountain, McClellan would defeat his enemy, but only after displaying a strong sense of self-preservation and a reluctance to commit reserve forces. His indecisiveness and reluctance would become a trademark weakness throughout his military career. It was not taken lightly by his commanding officers. Immediately following his first successful battle, McClellan's commander, William S. Rosecrans, bitterly complained that his attack was not reinforced as McClellan had agreed, and given the life-and-death nature of such a decision, questioned McClellan's honor and loyalty (Sears, 1988, pp. 90–91). To this day, there remain questions as to whether it was McClellan or his subordinates who were directly responsible for the majority of his success. Nevertheless, once again in the right place at the right time, these two minor victories propelled McClellan to national-hero status (Hiedler and Heidler, 2000, p. 1274). Then, in a stroke of luck and additional good timing, the *New York Herald* ran an article titled "Gen. McClellan, the Napoleon of the Present War" (Sears, 1988, p. 93).

The ensuing national notoriety further propelled McClellan, establishing his image as a strong, capable general who gets winning results in battle. Nevermind the battles he commanded were of little significance to the overall outcome of the Civil War. As was the case throughout his career, he was reaching levels of leadership at an exceptional, almost unrealistic pace. McClellan's newfound notoriety benefited him greatly, and shortly after the Union Army was defeated in the first Battle of Bull Run, his reputation preceded him, and he was once again courted for an even greater leadership role.

During the Battle of Bull Run, yielding to political pressure to engage, President Lincoln's Brigadier Gen. Irvin McDowell led his unseasoned Union Army across Bull Run against Confederate Brig. Gen. P. G. T. Beauregard. McDowell's ambitious strategy was to hit the Confederate Army with a surprise flank attack. Unfortunately, the timing of his attack was poorly executed by his officers and men. The poor execution and unintended extended time in battle allowed the Confederate reinforcements under Brig. Gen. Joseph E. Johnston to arrive from the Shenandoah Valley by railroad.

Johnston's troop arrival disrupted any momentum the Union Army had achieved during the initial battle at Bull Run. Making matters worse, a Confederate brigade of Virginians under the relatively unknown Brig. Gen. Thomas J. Jackson stood its ground, which resulted in Jackson receiving his famous nickname, "Stonewall Jackson." With the additional reinforcements, the Confederates launched a strong counterattack. The Union Army, having been outmaneuvered, began to hastily withdraw while under heavy fire. Additionally, the subconscious survival instincts and inherent self-preservation of the Union Army soldiers got the better of them, and the retreat turned into an all-out panic. McDowell's Union soldiers panicked and ran without order toward Washington, DC.

For President Lincoln, this was a huge blow to the Union's morale and required immediate action. After the Union's defeat at Bull Run on July 21, 1861, Lincoln summoned McClellan from western Virginia, where he had given the North the only engagements with any resemblance of victory, and where notoriety and fame made him the likely choice to replace McDowell.

Summoned by the president, McClellan traveled by special train on the main Pennsylvania line, traveling through Pittsburgh, Philadelphia, and Baltimore, and on to Washington, DC. Along the way, at each stop, McClellan would receive a hero's welcome. Carl Sandburg, an American writer, captured the moment when he wrote, "McClellan was the man of the hour, pointed to by events, and chosen by an overwhelming weight of public and private opinion" (Sandberg, 1942, p. 62).

In letters McClellan wrote to his wife, you can further observe his Hidden You personality traits and leadership genes. He wrote, "At every station where we stopped crowds had assembled to see the 'young general' . . . I could hear them say, 'He is our general' . . . I hope to thrash the infamous scamps before week over. All I fear is that I won't catch them . . . Well, it is a proud and glorious thing to see people here, looking up to me as their deliverer from tyranny . . . I realize now the dreadful responsibility on me—the lives of my men, the reputation of the country and the success of our cause . . . I shall feel my way and be very cautious" (Williams, 1991, p. 59).

Once in Washington, McClellan wrote, "I find myself in a new and strange position here, all deferring to me. By some strange operation of magic I seem to have become the power of the land . . . When I was in the Senate chamber today and saw those old men flocking around; when afterward stood in the library . . . and saw the crowd gather around to stare at me, I began to feel how great the task committed to me . . . who would have thought, when we were married, that should so soon be called upon to save my country? . . . I shall carry this thing *engrand* and crush the rebels in one campaign" (Williams, 1991, p. 60).

On July 26, 1861, the same day he reached the capital, McClellan was appointed commander of the military division of the Potomac, the main force responsible for the overall defense of Washington. Subsequently, on August 20, 1861, several military units in Virginia were consolidated under McClellan's command, prompting him to form the army he coined the Army of the Potomac, with himself as its first commander (Eicher and J., 2001, p. 372). As expected, McClellan reveled in his newly acquired power and influence, and in a letter to his wife wrote, "I almost think that were I to win some small success now I could become Dictator or anything else that might please me—but nothing of that kind would please me—therefore I won't be Dictator. Admirable self-denial" (Sears, 1988, p. 95).

Self-preservation intact, McClellan was still not content. He had successfully moved up another significant level of the leadership branch, yet his sights were clearly set on reaching the top. McClellan wrote, "I have no choice. The people call on me to save the country. I must save it, and cannot respect anything that is in the way. . . . I have no such aspirations. I would cheerfully take the dictatorship and agree to lay down my life when the country is saved" (Williams, 1991, pp. 60–61).

McClellan thrived in his new role, once again leveraging his strong logistical skills to organize his new army, while also using his charisma and charm to improve morale via frequent trips to the field, while also appealing to his troops' self-preservation. Through inborn survival instincts, men fear war and inherently fear death. McClellan's own fear and self-preservation were likely appreciated by the soldiers he led. He cared greatly for his men, and his reputation for being slow to accept battle was captured in the minds of those having to lead the way in battle.

In his new leadership role, McClellan was successfully readying his men, but he had not been truly tested while leading an army of this size. On his rapid ascent to the top, with no leadership journey, no systematic approach, a lack of mastery outside of war logistics, and no mentor to speak of, it was not long before the reality of war set in, where subconscious fear and anxiety wreak havoc, where the limbic system is in constant battle with the cerebral cortex. For McClellan, the greater responsibility and subsequent leadership duties started to have an effect on his self-preservation, and would soon start to cloud his judgment.

McClellan successfully created defenses for the US capital that were almost impenetrable, consisting of 48 forts and strong points with 480 guns manned by 7,200 artillerists (Sears, 1988, p. 116). His Army of the Potomac grew from 50,000 in July 1861 to 168,000 in November, becoming the largest military force the United States had ever raised (Sandberg, 1942, p. 62). In spite of his success in building a remarkable fighting force, recorded history has also shed light on his Hidden You and inability to "adapt." Any war, just like with silos and turf wars, has a high probability of inducing fear and anxiety that coincides with self-preservation, disrupting the decision-making process.

As tensions within high command continued to build, McClellan continued to demonstrate characteristics of an "alienated follower." He was unwilling to render humble service, expected a title for what he knew instead of what he had actually accomplished, and frequently disagreed on matters of strategy with Union leadership. Of great significance were his open and public disagreements with the general-in-chief, Lt. General Winfield Scott. McClellan rejected Scott's leadership tenets, favoring instead his own "Napoleonic style," a war strategy that consisted of building a sizable army capable of overwhelming the opposition in a grand battle. McClellan favored a style he had never put into practice. He proposed that his army should be expanded to 273,000 men and 600 guns to "crush the rebels in one campaign" (Sears, 1988, p. 98).

A driving force in McClellan's war strategies was his innate fear of failure and his conscious and subconscious reaction to overexaggerate the Confederate's strength. Throughout his tenure, he was always convinced the Confederate Army was ready to attack, which drove his obsession to build an army of greater force. McClellan's subconscious fears of failure would inhibit his cerebral analysis, which impacted his ability to confront reality through the need to "adapt." His lack of a systematic approach, his inability to establish common nomenclature among the group dynamics of his army, and his own innate fears paralyzed his ability to make critical decisions—especially when decisions required a quick and decisive course of action.

As an example, believing that the Confederacy had over 100,000 troops facing him, he declared a state of emergency in the US capital. McClellan made this decision based on his own reconnaissance. He did not confront reality, and he displayed a decision-making process that would suggest his fear of competition led to his self-inflicted leadership isolation and a silo decision-making process. It was through his leadership isolation that he incorrectly estimated 150,000 Confederate rebel soldiers were in position and ready to stage war.

As a result, McClellan's army became restless, and the outcome of his decisions alienated his followers and dismayed the leadership within the government. Historian and biographer Stephen W. Sears observed that McClellan's actions were "for the most part essentially sound" for a commander who was as outnumbered as McClellan thought he was, but McClellan in fact rarely had less than a two-to-one advantage over the armies that opposed him in 1861 and 1862. That fall, for example, Confederate forces ranged from 35,000 to 60,000, whereas McClellan's Army of the Potomac numbered 122,000 men and "by the end of the year . . . nearly 192,000" (Sears, 1988, pp. 104, 110). McClellan wrote, "I am here in a terrible place: the enemy have from three to four times my force . . . I can't tell you how disgusted I am becoming with these wretched politicians . . . I have a set of men to with unscrupulous and false; if possible they will throw whatever blame there is on my shoulders . . . I can't move without more means" (Williams, 1991, pp. 61–62).

Although McClellan was successful in building his army, his attitude toward existing leadership and his overtly cautious approach were having a profound impact on the overall group dynamics within his force and the highest levels of leadership. As a classic "alienated follower," McClellan isolated his decision-making process even further and withheld his plans from his leader, Lt. Gen. Winfield Scott. McClellan claimed he could not trust anyone in the administration to keep his plans secret from the press, and thus from the enemy.

Following the course of several disagreements about defensive forces on the Potomac River, McClellan wrote to his wife, stating, "I am firmly determined to force the issue with Genl Scott . . . a very few days will determine whether his policy or mine is to prevail—he is for inaction and the defensive. He endeavors to cripple me in every way . . . Hereafter the truth will be shown and he will be displayed in his true light" (Beatie, 2004, p. 241). Interesting perspective, as historical observation of McClellan's description of Lt. Gen. Winfield Scott is more likely to reflect McClellan's leadership than Scott's.

Whether he consciously or subconsciously applied Sun Tzu's *Art of War* tactic "If your opponent is temperamental, seek to irritate him," McClellan's dispute with his leader became increasingly personal. Lt. Gen. Scott became so irritated that he offered his resignation to President Lincoln, who, through recognition of his significant service to the country, refused to accept.

Timely rumors of McClellan resigning or instigating a military coup began to circulate. With the Union's morale in balance, and given McClellan's notoriety, Lincoln found himself in the middle of a turf war, standing in-between his two appointed leaders. One, a young, up-and-coming, ambitious leader who had managed to build a strong public reputation through the free press; the other, an elderly, self-transcending leader reaching the end of his glorious military career.

Lincoln's cabinet met and agreed to accept Lt. Gen. Winfield Scott's resignation. On November 1, he officially retired for "reasons of health" (McPherson, *Battle Cry of Freedom: The Civil War Era*, 1988, p. 360). At the age of seventy-five, to the outside world, it was a reasonable explanation. Lt. Gen. Winfield Scott had served his country well, having once been severely wounded in war, only to recover and assume his leadership position. He had not started as a strong leader, but through his leadership journey and the mastery of his trade, he was well respected by many at the time of his resignation.

Having demonstrated signs of leadership transcendence, it is highly probable that Lt. Gen. Winfield Scott had reached Maslow's needs of self-transcendence. He served on active duty as a general longer than any other person in American history, and historians have rated him as one of the most senior commissioned officers of all time. Some historians even rated him as the best American commander of his time. Over the course of his fifty-three-year career, Lt. Gen. Winfield Scott commanded forces in the War of 1812, the Black Hawk War, the Mexican–American War, the Second Seminole War, and the American Civil War. As previously written, it was his "Anaconda Plan" that was ultimately used to defeat the Confederacy, the same strategy that McClellan openly opposed. Lt. Gen. Winfield Scott served as commanding general of the United States Army for twenty years, longer than any other holder of the office. A man who unquestionably loved his country, a man whose integrity was respected by many, a man who was once described as a national hero after the Mexican–American War, was now being "left behind."

Despite lacking a leadership foundation, McClellan, through ambition and political savviness, reached the highest branch, and at the age of thirty-five became general-in-chief of all the Union armies. As is often the case for those whose ambition it is to reach the top, once there, his expectations were succeeded by the reality of having to actually fulfill the role.

As McClellan's responsibilities increased, so did the size of his army, as well as his growing reputation in respect to his own self-preservation and inherent fear of failure. This included his inability to commit to battle. Still in mass near Washington, Lincoln, as well as many other leaders and citizens of the Northern states, became increasingly impatient with McClellan's reluctance to attack the Confederate forces. The people's vote of confidence began to wane. Similar to today's "Generation Now," the Northern states wanted immediate favorable results. As a reflection of their own self-preservation—their fear of losing the war—they were beginning to question McClellan's leadership. Making matters worse, McClellan and his army would be defeated at the minor Battle of Ball's Bluff, thus adding to the overall fear, anxiety, and frustration of the Northern states. McClellan's positive reputation would turn negative.

In December of 1861, Congress formed the Joint Committee on the Conduct of the War, which became a significant challenge and distraction for many generals throughout the Civil War. This Joint Committee would often accuse the generals of incompetence, and in some cases, treason. McClellan was called as a first witness on December 23, but he presumably contracted typhoid fever and could not attend (Sears, 1988, p. 136). In his absence, his subordinate officers testified on his behalf, and by their own admission admitted to not having ever received any knowledge or specific plans regarding his war strategies. As is often the case within disorganized and stagnated teams, with McClellan as their leader, there were no instrumental qualities of enhanced communication applied. The result of this information created an echo chamber within the Joint Committee, where the belief that McClellan should be dismissed from his duties were amplified or reinforced.

As evidence of his growing insubordination, McClellan further damaged his reputation through his documented communications that depicted his view of his commander-in-chief, Abraham Lincoln. McClellan privately referred to Lincoln as "nothing more than a well-meaning baboon . . . the original gorilla" (McPherson, *Battle Cry of Freedom: The Civil War Era,* 1988, p. 364). McClellan's blatant lack of maturity, lack of discipline, disregard for authority, and most of all, his continued delay to enter battle became a bone of contention for President Lincoln. Similar to Schachter's study on rejection, the group dynamics of Lincoln's cabinet concluded that McClellan, now the "deviant," would not change or conform to the group. The group would eventually cease to communicate with McClellan. Additionally, as time progressed, group dynamics sought to isolate the "deviant" soldier, who came dangerously close to being "left behind."

Due to Lincoln's growing impatience and decreasing trust in McClellan's leadership, on January 10, 1862, he met with top generals in a private meeting. Lincoln purposefully excluded McClellan from the meeting, formally putting McClellan into leadership isolation. During the meeting, Lincoln directed his top generals to formulate a plan of attack, expressing his frustrations with the following remark: "If General McClellan does not want to use the army, I would like to borrow it" (McPherson, *Tried by War: Abraham Lincoln as Commander in Chief*, 2008, p. 66).

On January 12, 1862, McClellan was summoned to the White House, where the cabinet demanded to hear his war plans. Sensing disruption to his self-preservation, for the first time, McClellan revealed his strategy. However, he chose not to "adapt" and refused to give any specific details of the proposed campaign, afraid his plans would be shared with the enemy. Once again, disapproval of McClellan escalated. On January 27, Lincoln issued an order that required all his armies to begin offensive operations by February 22. On January 31, Lincoln issued a supplementary order for McClellan's Army of the Potomac to move overland to attack the Confederates, part of the Occoquan Plan Lincoln had been "pressing on McClellan since early December" (Sears, 1988, p. 149).

As expected, McClellan replied with a twenty-two-page letter objecting to the president's plan and advocating his own plan, what he called the "Urbanna Plan" (Sears, 1988, p. 149). The "Urbanna Plan" was the first written plan presented to President Lincoln by McClellan that provided a detailed strategy. Although Lincoln believed his plan was superior to McClellan's, he was shocked and relieved that McClellan finally agreed to share his plan. As a potential transcendent leader, Lincoln approved McClellan's plan, directing him to put his plan into immediate action.

Now ready to move forward, the weight of McClellan's past inaction and lack of maturity challenged his ability to successfully execute his "Urbanna Plan." In implementing his plan, McClellan experienced several unexpected failures, all attributable to his own self-described war strategies and his indecisiveness. The overall negative sentiment directed toward McClellan by both the Northern states and US government reached a peak, and Lincoln was served notice. On March 11, 1862, at a cabinet meeting, due to growing negative sentiment, Lincoln removed McClellan as general-in-chief by stating, "Major General McClellan, having personally taken the field at the head of the Army of the Potomac, until otherwise ordered, is relieved from the command of the other military departments" (Sears, 1988, p. 164). As a result, McClellan was "left behind." Until otherwise communicated, McClellan would only be responsible for the army he had originally built, the Army of the Potomac.

McClellan had reached the highest leadership branch, and like the "turkey" in the old wives' tale, his inability to "move" and "adapt" led to him being "left behind." Without Hidden You analysis, without a leadership foundation, it was just a matter of time. And the moral of the story for McClellan became reality: "Bullshit might get you to the top, but it will not keep you there!" Lincoln later described his decision to demote McClellan as a way to advert "the failure of the approaching campaign" (Sears, 1988, p. 165).

In his new role, again as the commander of the Army of the Potomac, McClellan went on to lead several battles, but he was never able to overcome his fear of failure, which plagued him throughout the Civil War. His inability to "move" and "adapt" led to self-inflicted struggles. He continued to overestimate the size of the Confederate Army, leading to an indecisiveness that ultimately plagued the Union Army's success.

McClellan's actions toward his own self-preservation began to take their toll. With no Hidden You knowledge and no leadership foundation, McClellan's limbic system took control. Under the pressures of war, McClellan succumbed to several mental breakdowns, in which fear led him to severe stress-induced depression and anxiety, and at times he was unable to function on a day-to-day basis.

During the Seven Days Battles, a series of six major battles over seven days from June 25 to July 1, 1862, near Richmond, Virginia, McClellan's fear peaked, and he chose "flight" instead of "fight," choosing to flee by distancing himself from the battlefields to escape his leadership responsibility. In the Seven Days Battles, Confederate General Robert E. Lee drove McClellan's Union Army of the Potomac away from Richmond and into a retreat down the Virginia Peninsula. In a telegram to Secretary of War Edwin Stanton, McClellan blamed the Lincoln administration for his reversals. "If I save this army now, I tell you plainly I owe no thanks to you or to any other persons in Washington. You have done your best to sacrifice this army" (Hiedler and Heidler, 2000, p. 1275). Fortunately for McClellan, Lincoln never actually received his inflammatory statement due to telegrapher censorship.

Broken, battered, and mentally in distress, in a strange and unexpected turn of events for McClellan, out of total desperation following the Union defeat at the second Battle of Bull Run, President Lincoln reluctantly returned to McClellan. Lincoln realized that McClellan was a strong organizer and a skilled trainer, and was able to pull together what remained of the Union Army after the second failed Battle at Bull Run. Still an "alienated follower," McClellan's inability to follow orders had contributed to the failure of the Union Army against the Confederates at the second Battle of Bull Run. Without this knowledge, on September 2, 1862, Lincoln named McClellan, now thirty-six, to again command "the fortifications of Washington, and all the troops for the defense of the capital." Once "left behind," McClellan was given the opportunity to "move" and "adapt." In the words of Henry Ford, "Failure is only the opportunity to begin again more intelligently."

McClellan's reappointment was not taken lightly. He would have a tough hill to climb, but certainly, with the right systematic approach, it represented an achievable task and an opportunity to learn from past failures. Similar to the Conduct of War Joint Committee, a new echo chamber was formed. This time, a majority of the cabinet members signed a petition declaring to the president "[their] deliberate opinion that, at this time, it is not safe to entrust to Major General McClellan the command of any Army of the United States" (Sears, 1988, p. 260), demonstrating just how far "left behind" McClellan had truly become. The president admitted it was like "curing the bite with the hair of the dog" (Bailey, 1984, p. 15). But Lincoln told his secretary, John Hay, "We must use what tools we have. There is no man in the Army who can man these fortifications and lick these troops of ours into shape half as well as he. If he can't fight himself, he excels in making others ready to fight" (Bailey, 1984, p. 15).

With a second chance, McClellan would once again prove successful in amassing the Union Army, and soon found himself leading men into battle once again. Unfortunately for McClellan, and as Frederick Douglass once said, "It is easier to build strong children than to repair broken men." A once prominent, confident, and ambitious young man, McClellan had been "left behind" and was now mentally broken. He was again in a leadership role with no systematic approach to draw upon.

The Battle of Antietam, McClellan's last commanding battle, was the single bloodiest day in American military history. The outnumbered Confederate forces fought valiantly. However, despite significant advantages in manpower, McClellan was unable to concentrate his forces to appropriately defeat his nemesis Gen. E. Lee. Instead, his indecisiveness provided Gen. Lee with the opportunity to shift his troops, prolonging the battle and allowing an eventual retreat.

Early in the Civil War, this type of retreat would signal a defeat. However, at this point, everyone was growing tired and impatient. As in the past, by overestimating the size of his opponent's army, McClellan was unwilling to employ his ample reserve forces to crush Gen. Robert E. Lee's army. Historian James M. McPherson has pointed out that the two corps McClellan kept in reserve were in fact larger than Lee's entire force. Although the battle was tactically inconclusive, Lee technically was defeated as he withdrew first from the battlefield and retreated to Virginia.

Following Gen. Lee's retreat, McClellan wired to Washington, "The enemy is driven back into Virginia. Maryland & Penna. are now safe" (Sears, 1988, p. 321). Although McClellan was admired in his own perceived success, those in Washington felt otherwise. Leaders in Washington were convinced that McClellan should have crushed Gen. Lee, who had a smaller army with its back to the Potomac River. In confronting reality, the leaders in Washington were right. McClellan certainly did not expose to those in Washington that during the Battle of Antietam, fear had struck again, and McClellan had fallen into a paralysis of indecision that clouded his judgment.

With lack of judgment, indecisiveness, and fear of failure, McClellan failed to pursue Gen. Robert E. Lee aggressively, and visibly prolonged the war. In response to his inaction, on November 5, 1862, Lincoln ordered McClellan be removed from command, and McClellan was once again "left behind" (Sears, 1988, p. 338). Following his removal, McClellan wrote to his wife, "Those in whose judgment I rely tell me that I fought the battle splendidly and that it was a masterpiece of art. . . . I feel I have done all that can be asked in twice saving the country. . . . I feel some little pride in having, with a beaten and demoralized army, defeated Lee so utterly. . . . Well, one of these days history will I trust do me justice" (McPherson, *Battle Cry of Freedom: The Civil War Era*, 1988, p. 545).

Following his death at age fifty-eight, a death of natural causes, the *New York Evening Post* commented, "Probably no soldier who did so little fighting has ever had his qualities as a commander so minutely, and we may add, so fiercely discussed" (Sears, 1988, p. 401).

To be fair, like all of us, McClellan had strengths and weaknesses. It was McClellan's Hidden You weaknesses that overpowered his strengths, preventing him from reaching true leadership transcendence. Although McClellan lacked the ability to apply many aspects of this systematic approach, most crucial was his inability to confront reality and his lack of realism. Without "star followers," he was unable to see or recognize anything for what it truly represented. Instead, he saw everything as he wanted it to be. This lack of realism led to his inability to take the appropriate actions against the enemy, which kept him and his followers from achieving many of their intended outcomes. His fear and self-preservation ultimately led to the unnecessary death of thousands of soldiers.

For most of us, having never faced the challenge of leading men and women into battle, it is only through the lens of history that such an observation can be derived, and we must respect and never lose sight of the gratitude owed to McClellan for his service. However, through the historical lens, in our quest of leadership observation, we too must confront reality. Historians have speculated that McClellan's indecisiveness, his fear of failure, and his inability to obtain decisive victories unnecessarily prolonged the Civil War. History has shown that the successful Civil War leaders did not fear failure; they learned to embrace failure as a form of success. These generals were willing to risk a major battle even when all preparations were not perfect. When "left behind," they learned to "move" and "adapt."

General William Tecumseh Sherman (1820–1891)

To provide an alternate perspective, next we will explore the leadership journey of William Tecumseh Sherman, who has been described as one of the great soldiers of the Civil War. As a respected leader and through his own leadership journey, Sherman came to understand various forms of leadership psychology—not through academics, however, but through personal experience and failure as a form of success.

Sherman was a realist, but how did he discover and apply this understanding to his leadership journey? How did he "move" and "adapt" to his Hidden You? Did he have a systematic approach to draw upon? How did his failures become success?

How would his leadership journey compare to that of McClellan? How can two individuals with similar experiences and leadership opportunities yield such vastly different profiles? To understand the answer to these questions, we will cross examine William Tecumseh Sherman.

Sherman was born in 1820 in Lancaster, Ohio (Williams, 1991, p. 7). His father, Charles Robert Sherman, was a successful lawyer who prior to his death sat on the Ohio Supreme Court. At the age of nine, Sherman's father died unexpectedly, creating great strain on their family system. Upon his death, Sherman's mother, Mary Hoyt Sherman, was now caring for eleven children with little to no money. To preserve the Sherman family, the young Sherman was taken into foster care by their Lancaster neighbor and family friend, attorney Thomas Ewing Sr. Sherman's other brothers and sisters would find refuge in other homes. From an early age, Sherman was already experiencing significant adversity.

Sherman's foster father, Thomas Ewing Sr., was an influential man in the community and, as a member of the political Whig party, he served as senator from Ohio and as the first secretary of the interior for the United States. Thomas Ewing Sr. would become a father figure for Sherman and played a significant role in Sherman's leadership journey. In the book *McClellan, Sherman, and Grant,* author T. Harry Williams described Sherman's leadership journey as one that consisted of "small successes, large failures, and frustrated ambitions" (Williams, 1991).

At the age of sixteen, with the help of his foster father, Sherman was accepted as a cadet in the United States Military Academy at West Point (Sherman, 1990, p. 14). While attending West Point, Sherman excelled academically, but he treated the demerit system with indifference. As a member of West Point during Sherman's attendance, William Rosecrans described Sherman as "one of the brightest and most popular fellows" and "a bright-eyed, red-headed fellow, who was always prepared for a lark of any kind, and who usually had a grease spot on his pants" (Hirshon, 1997, p. 13). In Sherman's own words, he described himself as "not considered a good soldier, for at no time was I selected for any office, but remained a private throughout the whole four years. Then, as now, neatness in dress and form, with a strict conformity to the rules, were the qualifications required for office, and I suppose I was found not to excel in any of these. In studies I always held a respectable reputation with the professors, and generally ranked among the best, especially in drawing, chemistry, mathematics, and natural philosophy. My average demerits, per annum, were about one hundred and fifty, which reduced my final class standing from number four to six" (Sherman, 1990, p. 16). During his time at West Point, Sherman demonstrated great ambition, however his journey toward leadership transcendence needed time to develop.

Sherman's Hidden You was ambitious. As a foster child, growing up in a house full of both biological and foster siblings, ambition was the catalyst for acceptance. Subconsciously, to protect his self-preservation and under the mentorship of his foster father, Sherman showed great respect, and in many ways was a "star follower" within the family system of his foster home. Sherman was eager to please, and it was this attitude that carried him into West Point.

At the age of twenty, two years before McClellan joined West Point, Sherman graduated with the class of 1840 and entered the army as a second lieutenant in the Third US Artillery, ordered to report to Governor's Island, New York Harbor. Sherman's first assignment required him to travel to Florida during the Second Seminole War against the Seminole tribe. Known as the Florida War, from 1835 to 1842, various groups of Seminoles came together to fight for their self-preservation in a turf war waged by the United States. Following several conflicts, the Florida War became known as the Seminole Wars. The Second Seminole War, often referred to as the Seminole

War, is regarded as "the longest and most costly of the Indian conflicts of the United States" (Lancaster, 1994, p. 18).

During Sherman's time in Florida, as second lieutenant, he commanded various detachments with as many as twenty men to carry out various responsibilities, such as safely escorting high-ranking officers and their families to various military locations. Following a United States victory, Sherman was reassigned and stationed in Georgia and South Carolina. As the foster son of Thomas Ewing Sr., a prominent politician, Sherman was able to use his relationship and family system associated with Thomas Ewing Sr. to engage within the upper circles of Charleston society (Hirshon, 1997, p. 21). The Old South society represented the rural, agriculturally-based, pre-Civil War economy and society in the Southern United States, consisting of Virginia, Maryland, North Carolina, South Carolina, and Georgia (Wikipedia, n.d.). Unlike McClellan, during Sherman's time in the army, he experienced little toward his leadership journey, and his ascent to the first branch of leadership took many years to achieve—an achievement that required little to no consumption of the now-dreaded bull dung along the way.

Following Sherman's uneventful assignment in the Old South, he was reassigned to the recently captured territory of California. Here he was tasked with performing mostly administrative duties. During this time, while many of his fellow soldiers saw action in the Mexican–American War, like most soldiers, Sherman became restless, eager to join the fighting.

While performing his duty in California, Sherman would be associated with a major event in history, but did not recognize the significance of his participation at the time. In 1848, Sherman was assigned to accompany the military governor of California, Colonel Richard Barnes Mason, in the inspection that officially confirmed that gold had been discovered in the region. This was the inauguration of the California Gold Rush. For Sherman, while the enormity of the event did not resonate at the time, they would later resonate through his memoirs. Toward the end of his service, Sherman earned a brevet promotion to captain for his service (Eicher and J., 2001). His promotion came without an increase in pay, and consciously or subconsciously, eventually led him to seek greater finances within civilian employment. Additionally, his lack of a combat assignment was discouraging and influenced his ultimate decision to resign from the army.

Sherman's perception at the time was not unlike what many experience today. With the absence of a Hidden You and no systematic approach, Sherman lacked an innate ability to recognize the extreme value and experience he had gained in California. It was during this time that he was exposed to a leader who resembled a transcendent leader. Sherman would describe Col. Richard Barnes Mason as a man of great intellect, who was not predisposed to take credit and who found delight in seeing others succeed. In his memoirs, he would describe Col. Mason as a leader who was capable of confronting reality, and who could only be described as interested in the self-preservation for all. It was through his interaction with Col. Mason that Sherman would be influenced by his first leadership mentor, the type of influence that would play a part in Sherman's leadership evolution.

Prior to his resignation, Sherman was sent back east with army dispatches that he was ordered to deliver in person to Gen. Winfield Scott. It was in the presence of Gen. Scott that Sherman would first hear of the real potential for civil war. Soon after providing the ordered dispatches, Sherman took a six-month leave of absence from the military, and on May 1, 1850, married Miss Ellen Boyle Ewing, daughter of the honorable Thomas Ewing Sr. (Sherman's foster father). Sherman and Ellen raised a family together, and like any parent who must provide for their family, he considered finances to be essential to a healthy family. Sherman would write in his memoir, "But the serious and greater question remained, what was I to do to support my family . . . all accustomed to more than the average comforts of life" (Sherman, 1990, p. 158).

In July of 1853, at the age of thirty-three, Sherman officially resigned his captaincy and accepted a position as the manager of the San Francisco branch of the St. Louis-based bank Lucas, Turner & Co. Sherman's role represented his first ascendance to the top of the fence post. And like the "turkey," it helped to get him out of harm's way, but not fully. Leveraging the private sector, Sherman would maintain Maslow's basic needs and find his ability to care for his self-preservation challenging. This was Sherman's first exposure to the need for a systematic approach to "move" and "adapt."

Accepting the opportunity to be a branch manager was the easy part. Getting back to California in one piece to begin his future line of work would prove to be a significant challenge. For Sherman, before his new career even started, finding success as a form of failure would take on new meaning. On his journey back to California, to further evaluate his potential new career opportunity, Sherman would suffer at the hands of two shipwrecks, and in his memoir he described having to float through the Golden Gate Bridge on the overturned hull of a foundering lumber schooner (Sherman, 1990, pp. 116–121). Adding insult to injury, Sherman would return to San Francisco at a time of great economic turmoil.

Having been in battle during the Seminole War, Sherman found himself battling a different kind of war within himself, a Hidden You war. Without today's technology, Sherman was not privy to today's broader understanding of our brain, our survival instincts, and our inborn fears. Whether it was barely surviving a journey back to California or the economic challenges he now faced, Sherman's natural reaction to fear was impacting his body's physiological response, and he began to suffer from stress-related asthma (Sherman, 1990, pp. 131–134, 166). In his memoir, reflecting on experience, Sherman wrote, "I can handle a hundred thousand men in battle, and take the City of the Sun, but am afraid to manage a lot in the swamp of San Francisco" (Royster, 1991, p. 134).

As part of bad timing, economic deficiencies required the San Francisco branch to be closed down, and for the first or second time—if you count being shipwrecked—Sherman was being "left behind." In May of 1857, Sherman was forced to close his branch and relocate to New York on behalf of the bank. Broken and defeated, still having not reached the next leadership branch, Sherman had to "move." Having begun the process to "move" and "adapt" to his unforeseen leadership predicament, Sherman found momentary fortune, as he was reassigned to the New York branch (Sherman, 1990, pp. 150–161) (Clarke, 1969, p. 318). Unfortunately, due to being in the wrong place at the wrong time, the financial Panic of 1857 once again led to financial deficiency and Sherman's New York branch was also forced to close.

The Panic of 1857 was caused by a declining international economy and an overexpansion of the domestic economy (International Publishers, 1986, p. xiii). Due to the interdependencies of the world economy in the 1850s, the financial crisis that began in late 1857 has been recognized as the first worldwide economic crisis. Once again, wrong place, wrong time, and Sherman was "left behind." He continued to work for the bank in different capacities, but he knew he would have to "move and "adapt" or he would find himself further "left behind."

In 1858, Sherman relocated to Leavenworth, Kansas, where he tried to find success through various ventures. He attempted to establish a law practice, and was unsuccessful. He tried other ventures, and was again unsuccessful. For Sherman, success was hard to find, yet he continued to "move" and "adapt," gaining tremendous knowledge and wisdom along the way. Although he remained on the fence post of leadership, the information and knowledge he gained during the early years of his leadership journey would serve him well later in life.

After failing at several different business ventures, in 1859, now at the age of thirty-nine, Sherman accepted the role of first superintendent of the Louisiana State Seminary of Learning & Military Academy in Pineville, which would later become Louisiana State University (History of LSU). As the first superintendent, Sherman was described as an effective and popular leader. Col. Joseph P. Taylor, the brother of the late President Zachary Taylor, stated, "If you had hunted the whole army, from one end of it to the other, you could not have found a man in it more admirably suited for the position in every respect than Sherman" (Hirshon, 1997, p. 68).

This was a remarkable compliment toward Sherman, and a peek into his potential for leadership transcendence. Up to this point, he had experienced much more failure than success. Yet, regardless of past failures, Sherman was recognized as a leader. Thus, without the requirement of bull dung, he was once again taking flight, and ascending to the next branch in his leadership journey. With success finally upon him, and the wind at his back, a different kind of "left behind" would ensue.

This time, Sherman would find himself in the right place at the wrong time. During this time, a great divide had overcome the United States between the Northern and Southern states. As a result, the Southern states invoked a secession. The Ordinance of Secession was drafted and ratified in 1860 and 1861 by each of the Southern states with the purpose of formally seceding from the United States of America (Wikipedia, Ordinance of Secession, n.d.). Through this process, each state ratified its own ordinance, typically by means of a special convention delegation or by a general referendum. The seceded states formed the Confederate States of America. In January 1861, as more Southern states seceded from the Union, the secession had reached Sherman. The Confederate States of America, which included the state of Louisiana—where Sherman was happily employed—issued him an edict to accept firearms surrendered to the state militia by the US arsenal at Baton Rouge, Louisiana, an act that would demonstrate his support of the Confederate States of America.

Sherman, in a place and in a job that for the first time he thoroughly enjoyed, was left with the decision to either "adapt" or be "left behind." Having experienced so many failures, he could not in good conscience represent the Confederates. Instead, he made a difficult personal decision to be "left behind." Sherman resigned and returned to the North. Prior to leaving, Sherman would write to the governor of Louisiana, stating, "On no earthly account will I do any act or think any thought hostile . . . to the . . . United States" (Hart, 1993, p. 64).

Although Sherman did not oppose slavery and sympathized with the Southern states, now the Confederate States of America, he vehemently opposed any attempt at dissolving the Union. On hearing of South Carolina's secession, and as a demonstration of true leadership realism, Sherman wrote to a good friend, a secessionist, "You people of the South . . . You don't know what you are doing . . . This country will be drenched in blood. . . . You are bound to fail. Only in your spirit and determination are you prepared for war. In all else you are totally unprepared, with a bad cause to start with" (Lewis, 1932, p. 138). Unlike McClellan, Sherman could see things for what they were, not what he wanted them to be.

Out of work, Sherman departed from Louisiana and headed straight to Washington, DC. Leveraging both family relationships and his own, Sherman was successful in arranging a face-to-face with Abraham Lincoln in the White House, and sought to influence the president with his insight. During their discussion, Sherman expressed concern about the North's state of preparedness (Sherman, 1990, pp. 185–186). However, the president, who was in the midst of his inauguration week, was courteous and kind, but had minimal listening skills due to all of the existing distractions.

Sherman needed a job, and through family and friends secured a respectable position as president of the St. Louis Railroad, a streetcar company. It was during this time that Sherman, from a distance and as a skeptic, watched the government hastily prepare for a civil conflict. Although he was now forty-one years old, Sherman's leadership journey still needed a solid foundation. In contrast to McClellan, Sherman had already experienced a lifetime of failure when compared to most. However, as with McClellan's success, Sherman's failures, adversity, subsequent fear and anxiety, and lack of a Hidden You analysis had not yet strengthened his resolve. Sherman's instinctive self-preservation and need for acceptance were in control. As a result, he would become frustrated with the North's inability to understand his communications about the Confederates of America being truly ready to fight, even to the death. Thus, his insight and visibility into the North was impacting his perception of the North's ability to succeed and prevail in the upcoming Civil War.

In his new job, Sherman was living in border-state Missouri as the secession crisis peaked. Out of frustration, he attempted to remain neutral. While trying to withdraw from the scenes, he observed firsthand the challenges and divide within Missouri, and what the state would endure after siding with the Union. However, during this time, there was a conflict within Sherman and an innate desire to participate and lead within this civil conflict.

Despite his outward communication and disinterest in the civil conflict, Sherman was actually quite willing and ready to accept a position within the Union Army. However, he preferred a smaller role, as he had grown tired of failure and uncertainty and was not convinced that the North was prepared. It is also possible that he subconsciously sought a lower rank as a safe haven for his self-preservation, and as a result of his many preceding failings, doubted himself as a leader.

In early April of 1861, Sherman declined an offer from the Lincoln administration to take a position as a major general of Volunteers Commission from Missouri and instead requested a lower grade in the regular army (Sherman, 1990, pp. 188–189). After learning of Union setbacks, his self-preservation caused a brief hesitation in his commitment to Union military service. Representing a potential "alienated follower," he ridiculed Lincoln's call for seventy-five thousand three-month volunteers to quell secession, reportedly saying: "Why, you might as well attempt to put out the flames of a burning house with a squirt-gun" (Bowman and Irwin, 1865, p. 25). However, in May of the same year, Sherman offered himself for service in the regular army, and through various connections, mainly his brother John Sherman, a Senator, was able to influence a commission and took the colonelcy of the Thirteenth Regular Infantry Regiment (Sherman, 1990, pp. 189–190) (Hirshon, 1997, pp. 83–86). As a result of his request to lead at a lower rank, and in his consumption of a minor portion of bull dung, Sherman would remain perched on the leadership fence post. Then, on June 7, 1861, he received a telegram summoning him to Washington (University of Notre Dame Archives, 1861).

As colonel of the Thirteenth US Infantry Regiment, a new regiment that Sherman would build, his first command would consist of a brigade of three-month volunteers (Sherman, 1990, p. 200). After little over a month, Sherman and his men found themselves in the first major battle of the Civil War, the first Battle of Bull Run. Going into battle, Sherman and his men were under the leadership of Brig. Gen. Irvin McDowell as part of the Army of Northeastern Virginia. The total number of Union troops on the ground was about thirty-five thousand, however, only about eighteen thousand troops were actually engaged. Sherman's infantry was part of the fighting.

During the First Battle of Bull Run on July 21, 1861, Sherman and his men were tested greatly. Several men lost their lives, and the eventual outcome represented a disastrous Union defeat.

Having already experienced various forms of defeat several times over, the defeat at Bull Run led Sherman to question his own judgment as an officer. Similar to McClellan, defeat and failure that fell upon the commanding officers would often lead to opportunity. On July 23, following the defeat of Bull Run and to help boost troop morale, President Lincoln visited the troops, and following his interaction with Sherman, having already been acquainted with him in the past, was extremely impressed. As a result, President Lincoln promoted him to brigadier general of volunteers (Hirshon, 1997, pp. 93–94). Additionally, the promotion included a seniority in rank to Ulysses S. Grant, Sherman's future commander and leadership mentor. Without consuming bull dung, and with no inherent ambition, Sherman would ascend to the first branch of his leadership journey. Before accepting his new leadership role, Sherman, in fear of rejection and failure, extracted a promise from President Lincoln that under no uncertain terms would he be asked to take over his newly assigned department. Sherman captured this desire by stating in his memoirs, "My extreme desire [is] to serve in a subordinate capacity, and in no event to be left in a superior command. He promised me this with promptness, making the jocular remark that his chief trouble was to find places for the too many generals who wanted to be at the head of affairs, to command armies, etc." (Sherman, 1990, p. 210).

Following his promotion, Sherman served under Maj. Robert Anderson as second in command in the Department of the Cumberland stationed in Louisville, Kentucky. Not long after settling into his new leadership role, Maj. Robert Anderson's health failed, rendering Anderson unable to lead. In an unexpected turn of events, Sherman succeeded Anderson in command of the department, clearly breaking the promise that Sherman believed he had extracted. Letting his inborn self-preservation and fear of failure get the best of him, Sherman telegraphed to

Lincoln, "I am ordered to command here. I must have a few experienced brigadiers. I will not be responsible for events but will do my best" (Williams, 1991, p. 168). Like McClellan, out of fear and rejection, Sherman concerned himself over the intelligence reports on the growing number of Confederate soldiers and would passionately request additional reinforcements. Sherman, while exuding passionate communication to include an abundance of projected nervousness, would capture the attention of Secretary of War Simon Cameron. Concerned for Sherman and his men, Simon decided to visit Sherman in Louisville for a face-to-face meeting to assess the request for reinforcement.

Unfortunately for Sherman, Cameron traveled with various representatives, including members of the free press. Like McClellan, Sherman was impacted by the press. However, unlike McClellan, Sherman found his representation to be far less favorable. During their discussion, Sherman's communication style and overall demeanor did not capture the heart and minds of the free press. His Hidden You and subconscious self-preservation got the better of him, and the audience noticed his nervousness. The free press wrote articles implying Sherman was an unfit leader.

The critical reports overwhelmed Sherman with fear and anxiety, causing him to lean on his own self-preservation and fear of rejection. In an exchange with the now general-in-chief of all the Union armies, Sherman wrote to none other than McClellan, and Sherman would insist on being relieved of his duties. With zero leadership transcendence to draw upon, McClellan acted as expected, and without hesitation replaced Sherman with Brig. Gen. Don Carlos Buell, and then transferred Sherman to St. Louis, Missouri, under the leadership of Maj. Gen. Henry W. Halleck.

In December, Sherman was put on leave after being considered unfit for duty. He would then travel to Lancaster, Ohio, to seek solace and overcome once again being "left behind." During his time in Lancaster, Ohio, concerned for his wellbeing, his wife, Ellen, sought advice from Sherman's biological brother, Senator John Sherman. In her letter, Ellen complained of Sherman's family system by stating, "Knowing insanity to be in the family and having seen [Sherman] on the verge of it in California, I assure you I was tortured by fears, which have been only in part relieved since I got here" (Williams, 1991, p. 177). Ellen would describe Sherman's mind as a "morbid state of anxiety" (Williams, 1991, p. 177).

Sherman later wrote to his brother, implying that his role as a commander "broke [him] down," and he admitted to contemplating suicide (Brooks and Jean, 1999, pp. 174, 176). His inability to apply Hidden You analysis was exponentially compounded when the *Cincinnati Commercial* described him as "insane" (*Cincinnati Commercial*, 1861). A few months would follow before the Union Army would give him another chance at an independent leadership role.

By mid-December 1861, Sherman had overcome his nervous breakdown and regained control of his once out-of-control limbic system. Feeling a need to re-engage and contribute to the war, Sherman was cleared to return to service. In March of the following year, Maj. Gen. Henry W. Halleck's command was redesignated the Department of the Mississippi and enlarged to unify command in the West. Halleck knew Sherman before the war and thought he could find a useful place for the now-recovered officer. Sherman's initial assignments were rear-echelon commands, where he would have to adapt to being "left behind." Under Maj. Halleck, who through transcendence wanted to help Sherman rebuild his reputation, suggested to General-in-Chief McClellan that Sherman be given command of an expedition on the Cumberland River.

Unfortunately for Maj. Gen. Henry W. Halleck, Sherman's reputation was still in the "echo chamber," and Secretary of War Edwin M. Stanton objected, telling Lincoln that any "expedition . . .

will prove disastrous under the charge of General Sherman" (Kennett, 2001, pp. 155–156). Sherman's self-preservation and Hidden You instincts certainly had a negative impact on his subconscious and conscious resolve. However, like most future transcendent leaders, he would find directional leadership journey guidance through strong mentorship.

Sherman was tasked with providing logistical support for the operations of Brig. Gen. Ulysses S. Grant. As the previous commander of the District of Cairo, Grant, who had just successfully commanded a major victory at Fort Henry and soon thereafter at Fort Donelson, was now in command of the District of West Tennessee. Sherman, having experienced so much failure and having been "left behind" on many an occasion, now showed signs of understanding the importance of following. Although Sherman was technically the senior officer at this time, as a humble leader he expressed to Grant his confidence in him and his willingness to be led by him.

Through this strong act of support, Sherman would become a loyal follower of Grant. In ensuing battles, Sherman, while forwarding troops on the front line, played critical roles in Grant's successful battles and joined Grant with a division of volunteers. Finding solace and guidance under Grant's leadership mentorship, on March 1, 1862, Sherman was assigned to Grant's Army of West Tennessee as commander of the Fifth Division (Eicher and J., 2001, p. 485).

This represented a significant turning point in his leadership journey. As Grant's "star follower," Sherman would once again ascend to the next leadership branch. Now on the "move" and as a "star follower," Sherman gained confidence in himself. Sherman was an exemplary follower and represented himself in positive, active ways and as an independent thinker. In battle, he was deft and decisive. Like his mentor, Sherman was fertile in counsel, yet did not blindly accept his leader's decisions or actions until evaluating them completely. No longer "left behind," Sherman was invoking a systematic approach of "move" and "adapt," and as a "star follower" had learned to succeed with and without a leader's presence.

In a form of "self-transcendence" and with self-preservation for all in mind, Sherman had come to recognize his leadership transformation and his appreciation for Grant's ability to connect, mentor, and provide guidance. In a letter to Grant, Sherman revealed his admiration for his leadership qualities by describing his strongest feature in his "simple faith in success" (Williams, 1991, p. 185). Recognizing Grant's understanding that failure is a form of success, Sherman wrote to Grant, "When you have completed your best preparations you go into battle without hesitation . . . no doubts, no reserve; and I tell you that it was this that made me act with confidence. I knew wherever I was that you thought of me, and that if I got in a tight place you would come—if alive" (Williams, 1991, p. 185). In recognition of his Hidden You and the importance of confronting reality, Sherman would write to a friend to describe Grant's leadership as follows:

"I am a damn sight smarter than Grant. I know a great deal more about war, military history, strategy, and grand tactics than he does; I know more about organization, supply, and administration, and about everything else that he does. But I tell you where he beats me, and where he beats the world. He don't care a damn for what the enemy does out of his sight, but it scares me like hell . . . I am more nervous than he is. I am more likely to change my orders, or to countermarch my command than he is. He uses such information as he has, according to his best judgement. He issues his orders and does his level best to carry them out without much reference to what is going on about him" (Williams, 1991, p. 187).

Together, in solidarity and for the self-preservation of all, Sherman and Grant would experience both success and failure, often being "left behind" only to once again "move" and "adapt."

At the Battle of Shiloh, Sherman was wounded twice—in the hand and shoulder—and had three horses shot out from under him. In what would become one of the most notable conversations of the war, Sherman said simply: "Well, Grant, we've had the devil's own day, haven't we?" After a puff of his cigar, Grant replied calmly: "Yes. Lick 'em tomorrow, though" (Walsh, 2005, p. 78).

Under Grant's leadership, Sherman proved instrumental to the successful Union counterattack at the Battle of Shiloh on April 7, 1862. Sherman's performance was exemplary and he was promoted to major general of volunteers (Eicher and J., 2001, p. 485). Albeit informal and without conscious cerebral analysis, Sherman had come to recognize his Hidden You, and as part of his inborn instincts had begun to "move" and "adapt" with a purpose. No longer was his limbic system controlling his leadership attributes. Sherman was beginning to display a systematic approach that would have a positive impact on his leadership evolution, one that was representative of a developing transcendent leader. Sherman had ascended to the next leadership branch.

The careers of both Grant and Sherman were ascending to greater heights, branch by branch. In Sherman's case, he had a great mentor and was a strong "star follower," and benefited greatly from Grant's leadership style and power persona during the two years they served together in the West. While fighting together in the Battle of Chickasaw Bayou, also called the Battle of Walnut Hills, in December of 1862, both men once again faced their fear of rejection through public opinion. The free press complained that the "army was being ruined in mud-turtle expeditions, under the leadership of a drunkard [Grant], whose confidential adviser [Sherman] was a lunatic" (Whitelaw, 1868, p. 387). In the past, under such ridicule and negative perception, Sherman would have let anxiety take control. However, his leadership journey, Hidden You analysis, and ability to "move" and "adapt" provided an adequate path toward realism and minimizing the probability of being "left behind."

Before the Battle of Chickasaw Bayou and what would later become known as the Vicksburg Campaign, Sherman expressed serious reservations about Grant's methodologies in preparing and executing in battle (Smith, 2001, pp. 235–236). As a "star follower," Sherman would provide strong guidance and influence Grant's decision-making process. Through Grant's guidance, Sherman would perform well in the Vicksburg Campaign. And under Grant's supervision, Sherman's performance did not go unnoticed. The historian John D. Winters in *The Civil War in Louisiana* (1963) describes Sherman's leadership journey by stating, "He had yet [before Vicksburg] to display any marked talents for leadership. Sherman, beset by hallucinations and unreasonable fears and finally contemplating suicide, had been relieved from command in Kentucky. He later began a new climb to success at Shiloh and Corinth under Grant. Still, if he muffed his Vicksburg assignment, which had begun unfavorably, he would rise no higher. As a man, Sherman was an eccentric mixture of strength and weakness. Although he was impatient, often irritable and depressed, petulant, headstrong, and unreasonably gruff, he had solid soldierly qualities. His men swore by him, and most of his fellow officers admired him" (Winters, 1963, p. 176).

The Vicksburg Campaign ended with a Confederate surrender on July 4, 1863. Now at the age of forty-three, and in honor of his leadership success, Sherman was given the additional rank of brigadier general in the regular army. Under Grant's leadership and command, and with Sherman's help as a subordinate, the Military Division of the Mississippi was now unified. Sherman would continue to grow as a leader. Under the most challenging circumstance that a leader can face, leading soldiers into battle, Sherman would continue to reflect the qualities of a "star follower" and continue to experience success in battle.

Following Grant's orders, Sherman successfully commanded several battles, even traveling by train to his posts per Grant's request. During this time, Sherman gained significant experience, and a form of battle "mastery" developed within his leadership attributes. Through his ability to "move" and "adapt," confront reality, live in the moment, and "thin-slice" situations and circumstances, Sherman made decisive and optimal decisions. Accepting failure as a form of success allowed him to transcend his previous leadership capabilities, where he was no longer just reactive. Sherman was becoming transcendent, and his cerebral analysis was allowed to think freely, without an assault from his limbic system. This would facilitate his ability to think with creativity and become a huge asset to both Sherman and the overall outcome of the Civil War.

Sherman admired Grant's confidence and took solace in his friendship. So when Grant's own success facilitated his ascent to the top, as a "star follower," Sherman too experienced an ascent. In the spring of 1864, President Lincoln promoted Grant, putting him in command of all the Union armies, ascending him to the very top of the Union Army. As a token of gratitude and respect, Grant appointed Sherman to succeed him as head of the Military Division of the Mississippi, putting him in total command of the Western theater of the war.

No longer afraid of being "left behind," and through his leadership evolution facilitated by a great mentor, Sherman had reached a level of leadership that resembled "mastery." Through his past failings and nervous breakdowns, with an ability to appreciate and learn from such experiences, Sherman had reached Maslow's need for "self-actualization." Sherman's leadership journey had led him to becoming a leader who, in spite of many failures, was now recognizing his full potential. Unlike McClellan's leadership evolution, Sherman's prepared him for the moment.

In what would become a defining moment in the Civil War and in Sherman's leadership legacy, he and his army marched toward Atlanta, Georgia. Sherman was now in command of three armies. They would fight a lengthy campaign known as the Atlanta Campaign. On September 2, 1864, Sherman and his army captured Atlanta, forcing the Confederates to retreat and abandon the city. As is often the case with transcendent leaders, regardless of how many times they are "left behind," the recognition that future success is sure to follow and the caring and feeding for the self-preservation of all lends itself to achieving intended outcomes.

Sherman's success in the Atlanta Campaign gained him significant notoriety. No longer did the free press nor the Northern states and its "echo chamber" describe Sherman as a lunatic. Now he was portrayed as a hero. The success of Sherman's Atlanta Campaign made him a household name, and it played a significant role in ensuring Lincoln's re-election in November of that same year (McPherson, *Tried by War: Abraham Lincoln as Commander in Chief*, 2008, pp. 231–250).

This campaign pitted Lincoln against none other than the Democratic candidate George B. McClellan. McClellan's defeat, or better described as McClellan once again being "left behind," was of great significance. Not only was Sherman's success impacting the state of the Civil War, his success would prove to be influential in the future of the United States of America. During this election, the Confederacy, as the Democratic party platform, called for peace negotiations based on the Union's acknowledgment of Confederacy independence. This made the capture of Atlanta, and McClellan's subsequent loss to Lincoln, a top candidate for Sherman's greatest leadership contribution to the Union cause.

Sherman's transcendent leadership qualities and his fulfillment of Maslow's "self-transcendence" can be observed following his success in Georgia. As a result of the positive coverage Sherman received, and with Grant having made little progress in his fight against Confederate Gen. Robert E. Lee's Army of

Northern Virginia, a bill was introduced into Congress to promote Sherman to Grant's rank of lieutenant general. Of greater significance was Congress's ambition to replace Grant with Sherman. In a show of gratitude and true transcendence, Sherman wrote to Gen. Grant vehemently repudiating the bill (Hart, 1993, p. 354). Sherman would go on record, showing his continued loyalty to Grant by stating, "General Grant is a great general. I know him well. He stood by me when I was crazy, and I stood by him when he was drunk; and now, sir, we stand by each other always" (Williams, 1991, p. 142).

Following the success of the Atlanta Campaign, the final campaigns of the Civil War ensued. Sherman's now-solid "mastery" of war leadership and his leadership transcendence would continue to influence Union success. Sherman, now using his creativity and war instincts, influenced Grant to allow him to march north through the Carolinas. Through his own understanding and real-world experience associated with life's many challenges, he came to recognize the magnitude that self-preservation has on individuals and society at large.

Seizing on the human instinct toward fear and self-preservation, Sherman's creativity would represent a new type of war, what Sherman would call "hard war." Sherman had a deep understanding and personal experience regarding fear, and how fear could paralyze an individual's psyche. Through this understanding, Sherman would destroy the Confederacy's strategic, economic, and psychological ability to wage war. In what would become known as "Sherman's March to the Sea," Sherman advanced his army through Georgia and South Carolina, ordering his army to destroy civilian supplies and infrastructure along the way.

The speed and efficiency of the destruction had a tremendous impact on the Confederate soldiers. Once word circulated of Sherman's path for destruction, Confederate soldiers abandoned their posts to protect their livelihoods back home. As part of

Sherman's strategy, he first concentrated his efforts in South Carolina, the first state to secede from the Union, anticipating the effect it would have on Southern morale (Woodworth, 2008, pp. 17–18, 320–321). Sherman's instincts were good, and the self-preservation of the Confederacy and its people began to crumble along its path.

That is not to lose sight of the avoided challenges and good fortune that would fall upon Sherman and his army. Sherman accurately anticipated his enemies' next moves. However, had the Confederate Army moved contrary to his expectations, the outcome could have been different. Sherman's boldness and ability to now face failure opened the door for his creativity and his ability to "adapt."

Sherman went on to capture the city of Columbia, South Carolina. Then Sherman continued marching his army, moving through North Carolina on what would ultimately become the longest march in the history of war. On March 21, Sherman's final significant military engagement was a victory over the Confederates at the Battle of Bentonville. Then, in late March of 1865, Grant's forces finally took Petersburg, Virginia, then captured Richmond, Virginia, that April, which led to Gen. Robert E. Lee's surrender of the Confederate Army, thus bringing an end to a long and bloody civil war.

Both Grant and Sherman continued to ascend to leadership levels that neither could have imagined. In 1869, Grant was newly elected and became president of the United States, and Sherman was appointed commanding general of the United States Army and promoted to general of the army—not bad for two leaders once described as a "drunkard" and a "lunatic."

SUMMARY

Just as in life, a leadership evolution is a journey with aspects that can only be obtained through experience and time. As we have observed through the lens of historical leaders, we can observe the leadership journey of individuals whose self-preservation and that of those they led rested solely on their shoulders. Through observing McClellan and Sherman, we can now recognize that the journey to leadership transcendence often starts down a similar path. It is only in how you observe and interpret your path that you can more effectively "move" and "adapt," and minimize being "left behind" while maximizing and appreciating the experience being "left behind" has to offer.

Through Hidden You analysis, you must first look within yourself and through personal discovery recognize how inborn survival instincts, the family system, and leadership genetics have shaped your personality. This will help you better recognize how your personality, innate communication skills, and subsequent social behaviors are interpreted through individual and group dynamics. Only through perpetual "move" and further developing your knowledge in the field of leadership psychology will you recognize how not only to adapt your Hidden You toward others, but also how to effectively connect with others. In doing so, you care for the self-preservation, instinctive needs, and quality of life that consciously and subconsciously all humans yearn to achieve.

By leveraging the basic tenets of biology and its association with leadership psychology through self-preservation and "survival of the fittest," you are able to better recognize when to "fight" or when to take "flight." The systematic approach to leadership transcendence provides common nomenclature for knowing when to "move," "adapt," and for being able to more effectively recognize being "left behind." Learning and applying the different elements of leadership is a process, not an event. Unlike a doctor during residency, there is no way to fast track this critical learning process. Learning how to "adapt" is essential to achieving stated goals. Regardless of your role, the opportunity to influence top down, bottom up, and inside out facilitates your ability to first learn how to be a "star follower." Through instrumental qualities of enhanced communication, you are able to more effectively "adapt" to both the strengths and weaknesses associated with your Hidden You. Along your leadership journey, you will experience human nature and the unintended consequences of social behaviors. You will be "left behind." In fact, if you are not being "left behind," then you are probably not leading. It is only through failure, and the instinctive need to vanquish and avoid the fear and anxiety that failure unleashes, that we learn most from our past experiences. Embrace failure, and recognize that failure is a form of success.

By applying the concepts of Hidden You and the systematic approach to leadership transcendence, you will ensure your leadership evolution is perpetual and with intent. It is only through your leadership journey that you will observe and learn from the many attributes identified and articulated in this book. It is through this understanding that you can better recognize our human instinct toward the need for self-preservation. As a transcendent leader, use this knowledge to embrace everything life has to offer, and most importantly, to know when and how to have fun. Leadership is not easy, and hierarchy will always be a reality. No one wants to fail, and the need for self-preservation is built into our DNA. Never stop moving, as "self-transcendence" is a purposeful beginning to a worthwhile life and a critical milestone toward achieving leadership transcendence.

REFERENCES

Ambady, N., & Rosenthal, R. (1992). "Thin Slices of Expressive Behavior as Predictors of Interpersonal Consequences: A Meta-Analysis." *Psychological Bulletin, 111 (2),* 256–274.

Bailey, R. H. (1984). *The Bloodiest Day: The Battle of Antietam.* Alexandria: Time-Life Books.

Beatie, R. H. (2004). *Army of the Potomac: McClellan Takes Command September 1861–February 1862.* New York: Da Capo Press.

Bowman, S. B., & Irwin, R. B. (1865). *Sherman and His Campaigns.* New York: Charles B. Richardson.

Bradberry, T. (2016, July 1). "10 Things You Do That Make You Less Likeable." *Entrepreneur.*

Brooks, S., & Jean, B. (1999). *Sherman's Civil War: Selected Correspondence of William T. Sherman, 1860–1865.* Chapel Hill: Univ. of North Carolina Press.

C. G., J. (1971). *Psychological Types (The Collected Works of C. G. Jung, Vol. 6).* Princeton University Press.

Cambridge, U. o. (2014, February 11). "Males and females differ in specific brain structures." *ScienceDaily.*

Carney, D. R., Colvin, C. R., & Hall, J. A. (2007). "A thin slice perspective of accuracy of first impressions." *Journal of Research in Personality, 41,* 1054–1072.

Cincinnati Commercial. (1861, December 11).

Clarke, D. L. (1969). *William Tecumseh Sherman: Gold Rush Banker.* San Francisco: California Historical Society.

Coffield, F., Moseley, D., Hall, E., & Eccelstone, K. (2004). *Learning styles and pedagogy in post-16 learning: a systematic and critical review.* London: Learning and Skills Research Center.

Colcombe, S. J., Erickson, K. I., Scalf, P. E., Prakash, R., McAuley, E., Elavsky, S., . . . Kramer, A. F. (2006). "Aerobic Exercise

Training Increases Brain Volume in Aging Humans." *Journal of Gerontology, 61A(11)*, 1166–1170.

Colcombe, S., & Kramer, A. F. (2003). "Fitness effects on the cognitive function of older adults: A meta-analytic study." *Psychological Science, 14(2)*, 125–130.

Craddock, M. (2011). *Power Genes: Understanding Your Power Persona.* Harvard Business School Publishing.

Cronbach, L. (1955). "Processes Affecting Scores on 'Understanding Others' and 'Assumed Similarity.'" *Psychological Bulletin,* 52(3), 177–193.

Dess, G. G., & Picken, J. C. (2000). "Changing Roles: Leadership in the 21st Century." *Organization Dynamics, 28 (3),* pp. 18–34.

DeWall, C. N. (2011). "Social Acceptance and Rejection: The Sweet and the Bitter." *Current Directions in Psychological Sciences,* 20, 256–260.

Drubach, D. (2000). *The Brain Explained.* New Jersey: Prentice Hall.

Duncan, W. J., & Dodds, P. S. (2007). "Influentials, Networks, and Public Opinion." *Journal of Consumer Research, 34 (4)*, 441–458.

Eicher, J. H., & J., E. D. (2001). *Civil War High Commands.* Stanford: Stanford University Press.

Fadden, H. (2014, June 14). *glossophobia-fear-public-speaking.* Retrieved from health-benefits-of.net: http://health-benefits-of.net/glossophobia-fear-public-speaking.

Fager, R., & Fadiman, J. (2005). *Personality and Personal Growth (6th ed.).* New York: Pearson Practice Hall.

Federation of American Societies for Experimental Biology. (2014, April 27). "Fight memory loss with a smile (or chuckle)." *ScienceDaily.*

Forsyth, D. R. (2010). *Group Dynamics (5th Edition).* Belmont: Wadsworth.

Gladwell, M. (2005). *Blink.* New York: Hachette Book Group.

Gladwell, M. (2008). *Outliers.* New York: Hackette Book Group.

Goffee, R., & Jones, G. (2000). "Why Should Anyone Be Led By You?" *Harvard Business Review.*

Green, S. (1998). *The 48 Laws of Power.* Penguin Group.

Griffen, L. (2012, October 18). *The Secret Powers of Middle Children.* Retrieved from *Psychology Today: 74.* https://www.psychologytoday.com/blog/field-guide-families/201210/the-secret-powers-middle-children.

Hamlin, K. J. (November 2007). "Social Evaluation by Preverbal Infants." *Nature,* 557–559.

Hart, L. B. (1993). *Sherman: Soldier, Realist, American.* New York: Da Capo Press.

Hebb, D. (1949). *The Organization of Behavior.* New York: Wiley and Sons.

Heyn, P., Abreu, B. C., & Ottenbacher, K. J. (2004). "The effects of exercise training on elderly persons with cognitive impairment and dementia: A meta-analysis." *Archives of Physical Medicine and Rehabilitation, 85(10),* 1694–1704.

Hiedler, D. S., & Heidler, J. T. (2000). *George Brinton McClellan. In Encyclopedia of America Civil War: A Political, Social, Military History.* (D. S. Heidler, & J. T. Heidler, Eds.) New York: W.W. Norton & Company.

Hill, D. T., & Russell, I. (2013). *Blessed Beyond Measure.* CreateSpace Independent Publishing Platform.

Hill, N. (1928). *The Law of Success.* Meriden: Ralston University Press.

Hill, N. (1937). *Think and Grow Rich.* Meriden: Ralston Society.

Hirshon, S. P. (1997). *The White Tecumseh: A Biography of General William T. Sherman.* John Wiley & Sons.

History of LSU. (n.d.). Archived March 10, 2009.

International Publishers. (1986). *Collected Works of Karl Marx and Frederick Engels* (Vol. 28). New York: International Publishers.

Jung, C. (1953). *Psychiatric Studies. The Collected Works of C.G. Jung Vol 1.* Princeton University Press.

Kaufman, S. B. (2011, November 8). "Why Inspiration Matters." *Harvard Business Review.*

Kelley, H. H. (1967). Attribution Theory in Social Psychology. In D. Levine (ed.). *Nebraska Symposium on Motivation.*

Kelley, H. H. (1971). *Attribution In Social Interaction.* New York: General Learning Press.

Kelley, H. H. (1972). *Casual Schemata and the Attribution Process.* New York: General Learning Press.

Kelley, H. H. (1973). "The Process of Causal Attribution." *American Psychologists*, 28(2), 107–128.

Kelley, R. (1988). "In Praise of Followers." *Harvard Business Review*, pp. 66, 142–148.

Kennett, L. (2001). *Sherman: A Soldier's Life.* New York: HarperCollins.

Kerr-Dineen, L. (2010, November 8). "Want to know your odds for a hole-in-one? Well, here they are." *Golf Digest*.

Lancaster, J. (1994). *Removal Aftershock: Seminoles Struggles Survive West* (1st ed.). Knoxville: University of Tennessee Press.

Larson, S., & Nordvall. (2010). *Study Circles in Sweden: An Overview with a Bibliography of International Literature.* Linkoping: Linkoping University Electronic Press.

Leonard, G. (1992). *Mastery.* New York: Plume.

Lewis, L. (1932). *Sherman: Fighting Prophet.* New York: Harcourt Brace & Company.

Liddell, H. (1993). *Sherman: Soldier, Realist, American.* Da Capo Press.

Macmillan Encyclopedia of Physics. (1996). *Physics of Body.* New York.

Maslow, A. H. (1943). A Theory of Human Motivation. *Psychological Review*, 50(4): 370–396.

Maslow, A. H. (1954). *Motivation and Personality.* New York: Harper.

Maslow, A. H. (1987). *Motivation and Personality.* New York: Longman.

McClelland, D. (1987). *Human Motivation.* New York: Cambridge University.

McClelland, D. C. (1961). *The Achieving Society.* Princeton: Van Nostrand Co.

McClelland, D. C. (1978). "Managing Motivation to Expand Human Freedom." *American Psychologist, 33 (3)*, 201–210.

McPherson, J. M. (1988). *Battle Cry of Freedom: The Civil War Era.* New York: Oxford University.

McPherson, J. M. (2008). *Tried By War: Abraham Lincoln as Commander in Chief.* New York: Penguin Press.

Murray, H. A. (1938). *Explorations in Personality.* New York: Oxford University Press.

Myers, I. (1980). *Gifts Differing: Understanding Personality Type.* CPP, Inc.

Myers, I. B. (2003). *MBTI Manual: A Guide to the Development and Use of the Myers-Briggs Type Indicator.* Moutainview: CCP.

Pendersen, D. M. (1965). "The Measurement of Individual Differences in Perceived Personality-Trait Relationship and Their Relation to Certain Determinants." *The Journal of Social Psychology,* 65, 233–258.

Phillips, B. (1974). "He wows them at K-Wesleyan." *The Salina Journal,* 18.

Rafuse, E. S. (2005). *McClellan's War: The Failure of Moderation in the Struggle for the Union.* Bloomington: Indiana University Press.

Royster, C. (1991). *The Destructive War: William Tecumseh Sherman, Stonewall Jackson, and the Americans.* New York: Knopf.

Ruigrok, A. N., Salimi-Khorshidi, G., Lai, M.-C., Baron-Cohen, S., Lombardo, M. V., Tait, R. J., & Suckling, J. (2013). "A meta-analysis of sex differences in human brain structure." *Neuroscience & Biobehavioral Reviews.*

Sandberg, C. (1942). *Storm Over the Land: A Profile of the Civil War.* New York: Harcourt Brace and Company.

Schacter, S. (1951). "Deviation, Rejection, and Communication." *The Journal of Abnormal and Social Psychology, 46 (2),* 190–207.

Schoen, M. (2013). *Your Survival Instinct is Killing You.* New York: Hudson Street Press.

Schumann, K. (2011). *The Secret Power of Middle Children.* Penguin.

Sears, S. W. (1988). *George B. McClellan: The Young Napoleon.* New York: Mifflin Harcourt Publishing.

Sherman, W. T. (1990). *Memoirs of General W.T. Sherman* (2nd ed.). New York: Literary Classics of the United States.

Skojec, S. (2016, March 30). "We Must Pray for the Dead, Even the Holy." *One Peter 5.*

Smith, J. E. (2001). *Grant.* New York: Simon & Schuster.

Speech in the House of Commons. (1916, May 17). Royal Assent.

Srivastava, S., Guglielmo, S., & Beer, J. (2010). "Perceiving Others' Personalities: Examining the dimensionality, assumed similarity to the self, and stability of perceiver effects." *Journal of Personality and Social Psychology*, 98(3), 520–534.

Sutton, R. (2007). *The No Asshole Rule.* New York: Grand Central Publishing.

Tebow, T. (2016). *Shaken: Discovering Your True Identity in the Midst of Life's Storms.* Colorado Springs: Water Brook.

Thomas, H. (1997). *False Impressions.* New York: Touchstone.

Tzu, S., & Giles, L. (2009). *The Art of War.* The Floating Press.

University of Notre Dame Archives. (1861).

Vedantam, S. (2010). *The Hidden Brain.* Speigel & Grau.

Walsh, G. (2005). *Whip the Rebellion: Ulysses S. Grant's Rise to Command.* New York: Forge Books.

Wesselman, E. D. (2014). "Revisiting Schacter's Research on Rejection, Deviance, and Communication (1951)." *Social Psychology, 45(3)*, 164–169.

Whitelaw, R. (1868). *Ohio in the War: Her Statesman, Her Generals, and Soldiers.* New York.

Wikipedia. (n.d.). "Leadership Psychology." Retrieved from Wikipedia: https://en.wikipedia.org/wiki/Leadership_psychology.

Wikipedia. (n.d.). "Old South." Retrieved from Wikipedia: https://en.wikipedia.org/wiki/Old_South.

Wikipedia. (n.d.). "Ordinance of Secession." Retrieved from Wikipedia: https://en.wikipedia.org/wiki/Ordinance_of_Secession.

Wikipedia. (n.d.). "Pacific Railroad Surveya." Retrieved from Wikipedia: https://en.wikipedia.org/wiki/Pacific_Railroad_Surveys#cite_ref-winter_2-1.

Wikipedia. (n.d.). "Thin-slicing." Retrieved from Wikipedia: https://en.wikipedia.org/wiki/Thin-slicing#cite_note-2.

Wikipedia. (n.d.). "William Blake." Retrieved from Wikipedia: https://en.wikipedia.org/wiki/william_blake.

Williams, H. T. (1991). *McClellan, Sherman, and Grant.* Rowman & Littlefield.

Willingham, D. T., Hughes, E. M., & Dobolyi, D. G. (July 2015). "The Scientific Status of Learning Styles Theories." *Teaching of Psychology*, 42 (3): 266–271.

Winston, R. (2002). *Human Instinct.* London: Bantam.

Winters, J. D. (1963). *The Civil War in Louisiana.* Baton Rouge: Louisiana State University Press.

Woodworth, S. E. (2008). *Grant's Lieutenants: From Chattanooga to Appomattox.* Lawrence: University of Kansas Press.

Zenger, J. (2013, June 13). "The Unlikable Leader: 7 Ways To Improve Employee/Boss Relationships." *Forbes*.

ABOUT THE AUTHOR

Photograph by Margaret Walsh

John B. Slone is an IT executive focused on sharing his vast knowledge and experience to help future leaders reach leadership transcendence. As an entrepreneurial thinker with an insatiable curiosity, John has spent the last twenty years understanding leadership.

Having managed from within all levels of both small and large companies, including operations and sales organizations, John has been thoroughly exposed to the many complexities associated with our social evaluation process and how our innate social behaviors influence success or failure.

John currently resides in Jensen Beach, Florida, where he lives with his family, enjoying all the outdoor activities Florida has to offer.

John Slone, author of *The Hidden You and Your Leadership Evolution,* has partnered with Ridgeline Coaching. Ridgeline Coaching is dedicated to helping leaders grow and connect more powerfully with their leadership strengths and their teams. We are pleased to be offering The Leadership Evolution workshop. This is an interactive session where participants will dive deeper into the materials presented in the book and work on ways to incorporate a systematic approach to their own leadership growth and development. For more on the workshop or to book a workshop for your organization, please contact us at www.RidgelineCoaching.com.